# BIG
# MONEY
## LITTLE EFFORT

# BIG
# MONEY
# LITTLE EFFORT

A Winning Strategy for
Profitable Long-term Investment

# Mark Shipman

KOGAN
PAGE

London and Philadelphia

First published in Great Britain and the United States in 2008 by Kogan Page Limited

120 Pentonville Road
London N1 9JN
United Kingdom
www.koganpage.com

525 South 4th Street, #241
Philadelphia PA 19147
USA

© Mark Shipman, 2008

ISBN 978 0 7494 4943 8

**British Library Cataloguing-in-Publication Data**

A CIP record for this book is available from the British Library.

**Library of Congress Cataloging-in-Publication Data**

Shipman, Mark.
    Big money, little effort : a winning strategy for profitable long-term investment / Mark Shipman.
        p. cm.
    Includes bibliographical references and index.
    ISBN 978-0-7494-4943-8
    1.  Investments.  2.  Speculation.   I. Title.
    HG4521.S5245    2008
    332.6--dc22

                            2007043624

Typeset by Saxon Graphics Ltd, Derby
Printed and bound in Great Britain by MPG Books Ltd, Bodmin, Cornwall

*I dedicate this book to my family for their love and their continued support and encouragement for everything I do.*

# Contents

*About the author*  *xi*
*Preface*  *xiii*
*Acknowledgements*  *xv*

**Introduction**  **1**

**1 But why bother?**  **7**

**2 Be careful who you trust**  **9**
Fund managers 10; Brokers/analysts 11; Tied advisers 12;
Independent financial advisers 13; Other professionals 13

**3 How to spot the friend from the foe**  **15**

**4 You can beat the professionals**  **21**

**5 But...**  **25**
A failure to set goals 26; A failure to plan 28; Assumption 30;
Procrastination 31; Requiring perfection 32; Trying to buy
the lows and sell the highs 33; Allowing your emotions to
control your investment decisions 34

**6 Systematic investing**  **37**

**7 The benefits of evaluating a system**  **41**

8  Disciplined market timing                                    45

9  Market timing vs buy and hold                                47

10  The psychology of following a system                        59

11  Is that all there is?                                       63

12  The Turtles                                                 67

13  The Long-Term Investment System                             71
    Moving averages 72

14  The rules                                                   75

15  An operational guide                                        77

16  Where to invest – asset allocation                          87
    Stock market index timing 91; Individual stocks and
    shares or sectors 97; How much? 101

17  The major stock market indices                             103
    The Standard & Poor's 500 Composite Index
    (United States) 103; The Dow Jones Industrial Average
    (United States) 111; The NASDAQ-100 Index (United
    States) 112; The FTSE 100 Index (United Kingdom) 114;
    The DAX 30 Index (Germany) 115; The CAC 40 Index
    (France) 116; The Nikkei 225 Index (Japan) 117;
    The Hang Seng Index (Hong Kong) 121

18  The System – historical performance 1951–2007              123
    S&P 500 Composite Index historical record 123;
    S&P 500 Composite Index historical performance
    summary 145

19  The 1987 Crash                                             149

20  Conclusion                                                 153

*Appendix A: Useful contacts*                                  157
*Appendix B: Stock market index investment products*           159
*Appendix C: Top 20 largest stock exchanges*                   161
*Glossary of financial terms*                                  163
*References and further reading*                               169
*Index*                                                        171

# About the author

Mark Shipman is a highly successful investor, having made a personal fortune from backing his own judgement with his own money, and along with legends such as Warren Buffett and George Soros he is listed as one of *Global Investor*'s Top 100 Investment Experts.

He was born in England in 1962 and, following an uninspiring education, left school at 16 with minimal qualifications to join the ranks of the unemployed. Shortly before his 17th birthday, he obtained a job working in the post room of an Australian bank in the City of London and within a few months he was transferred to the accounts department. Following a series of promotions, Mark's career path changed when he was offered a position in the dealing room, where he specialized in the trading of futures contracts and in the research, development and application of proprietary trading systems.

In 1990, having borrowed money from friends and family, Mark left the City to establish his own hedge fund management company, the first to seek independent regulation in the United Kingdom. The following year he achieved personal success by winning the World Professional Futures Trading Championship, and by 1993 he was considered one of the leading money managers in the world (source: *Futures and Options World*).

Mark retired from fund management in 1996 at the age of 33 to concentrate on managing his own money and to pursue a number of interests and hobbies. Nowadays, as well as continuing to participate in long-term investment trends, he consults to a select group of City institutions, is a sought-after keynote conference speaker, has written numerous newspaper and magazine articles, and makes regular guest appearances on the Sky News and CNBC television channels and on BBC Radio. In addition, he is the author of the ground-breaking investment book and number one best-seller *The Next Big Investment Boom*.

Away from the world of finance, he is an accomplished tournament poker player and a successful racehorse owner/breeder, with his distinctive maroon and light blue racing colours recently carried to victory in one of Europe's richest races.

For more information visit www.trend-follower.com.

# Preface

My grandfather was born and brought up in Victorian England in the early part of the last century. He worked for the council as a road sweeper and rented a terraced house in West Ham, a working-class borough in east London. Very much a product of Victorian education and values, my grandfather knew his place in life and in the social order. Like the vast majority of his generation, he was never likely to accumulate any serious assets or money, and his main focus was just to survive and provide for his family.

His children, my father and aunts, and his grandchildren, myself included, find themselves in a very different and more fortunate position. Since the end of the Second World War, Western economies have been in a period of economic growth not seen before in modern history. Wealth creation via better wages, pension provisions and an exponential increase in home ownership and house price values has afforded many people with a financial prosperity that past generations could only have dreamt about. In fact, never before have so many people had so much control over such large amounts of money.

However, this has created a problem: our education system has failed to keep pace. My parents, myself and my daughter were and are still taught the usual subjects such as maths and English, just as my grandfather was, but there is an essential life skill that has never been and still isn't taught to the masses: how to manage, control and invest money to protect and provide for your financial future. The upper, ruling classes have always had access to good financial education and advice, but the majority sitting beneath them, on the lower rungs of the ladder, now have the money but lack the knowledge. Such a condition leads to a number of unpleasant outcomes, including mismanagement and exploitation by those in the financial services industry who should know better, which could result in lost opportunities to grow and enjoy this new-found wealth. You've worked hard for it and you deserve to enjoy it, but typically a lack of sound financial education leads to poor investment decisions, which in turn result in losing money.

My intention is to rectify this situation. Through the publication of my books and my media, lecture and seminar appearances, I'm hoping to redress the imbalance and impart some of my experience and knowledge about investing to those who are interested. I myself received no formal education in the mechanics of managing money, but I made the effort to learn, and I'm truly thankful to the handful of successful investors who decided to become authors and impart their knowledge via books. My entire career and fortune began with ideas, recommendations and information gleaned from other people, and now it's my turn to pass on my own experience. Understanding how money and the financial markets work and how you can exploit investment trends and increase your own wealth is not as difficult as some would have you believe. That's why the books I write are not that long in length. Why use 500 pages when less than half that amount will get the message across? I don't want to fill your head with jargon or theories; I just want to teach you how I operate and then the choice of whether or not you want to use that information is yours.

# Acknowledgements

There a number of special people to whom I owe a major debt of gratitude for their help, advice and timely support throughout my career in finance, fund management and investing. I am eternally grateful to (in alphabetical order): Rupert Allan, Phil Bellanti, Frank Burgess, Allen Cheng, Steve Ciampi, Brian Cornell, Carol Dickman, Sandra D'Italia, Sean Doyle, David Elkin, Frank Franiak, Dick Grace, James Green, Karl and Barbara Gysin, Mike Harkins, Matt Johnson, Richard Kovner, Ashley Levett, Melvin Mardell, Nicola Meadon, Bill O'Heron, Jeremy Parfit, Lois Peltz, Scott Ramsey, Mike Schaefer, Gerry Sharma, Grace and Bill Sullivan, Ray Thompson, Fritz and Elle Uthe, and Rose and Bill Young.

Also, special thanks once again to Equis International Inc of Salt Lake City, Utah (www.equis.com), for allowing me to reproduce their excellent Metastock software charts, and to Bill Muller of Paritech (www.paritech.co.uk) for his kind help and assistance with the programming.

# Introduction

When I left the City of London in 1990 to start my own hedge fund management company, the first such business to apply for independent regulation in the United Kingdom, I was conscious of the fact that many of my competitors in the United States had developed and operated mechanical systems to speculate in the markets. The benefits for a fund management company to operate systematic approaches were twofold.

Firstly, a mechanical system with clear fixed rules for entering and exiting positions could be tested on past market data, not only to prove its historical profitability but to identify other performance characteristics such as volatility, profit and loss profiles, drawdowns and the systems reaction and profitability to exogenous events like presidential assassinations, terrorist attacks and currency crises to name but a few. Not only did this provide my company with detailed information about the cornerstone of our business, the profitability of our methods, but it also provided prospective clients with the same statistics. Such detailed past performance analysis, combined with an explanation of exactly what market conditions would create both good and bad returns, helped prospective clients to decide whether or not they wanted to invest, which provided us with a serious marketing advantage over more discretionary fund managers, who just couldn't offer such statistics.

Secondly, with the advent of powerful affordable computers, we could research, develop and operate mechanical trading and investing systems with minimal staff. There was no need for vast office space packed full of research analysts, which meant our business operating costs could be kept very low compared to traditional fund management companies, enabling us to offer very attractive portfolio management fees. I had been successfully using systematic trading and investing whilst in the City and therefore for me it was an easy decision to focus the market speculation side of my new fund management business towards using systems. Although at the time systematic trading and investing was not a new concept, the majority of fund management companies utilizing such systems were based in the United States, which enabled my business to become one of the first in Europe to use such an approach. This fact, combined with some very strong performance numbers, enabled me to grow my business into one of the top alternative fund management companies in the world in the space of just three years.

Systematic trading and investing has been at the core of my career in market speculation ever since and, although nowadays I've added elements of discretion to some of those approaches as detailed in my first book, *The Next Big Investment Boom*, I still operate a couple of rigid systems with clearly defined entry and exit signals. Following the publication of my first book, I became inundated with requests from readers to reveal more of my methods and, in particular, the more systematic strategies. So, to satisfy the demand, I decided to write this book and reveal one of my simple, ultra-long-term systems for investing in the stock market.

It is a pure system with clear, identifiable entry and exit signals, and if you follow the rules as instructed you will establish and liquidate your positions on exactly the same day and at around the same market level as I do. Do not be misled by the apparent simplicity of the System. Its performance over the last 20 years is far superior to that of the majority of the fund management industry, and this is in addition to a further 30 years of positive results from the historical testing we undertook on behalf of my hedge fund management company. Unimaginatively I've decided to call it 'the Long-Term Investment System', which should tell you all you need to know about the focus of the approach. It is a mechanical system in the sense that, once you have read and understood its simple rules, you will conduct the weekly analysis and generate exactly the same signals as everyone else who operates it, myself included. I've held nothing back; the rules in this book are the same rules that I use for investing a percentage of my own money.

Readers who've bought my first book will be aware that the main focus of my investing relies upon 'stage analysis' of the current long-term fundamentals. Then, once a potential asset class has been identified, I apply a simple set of technical (price chart-based) criteria that have to be met before I invest. Using this approach, I typically participate in five or more different positions, spreading my capital and hopefully some of the risk. All this analysis is conducted just once a week, and positions are established or liquidated at the beginning of the following week.

In contrast, the Long-Term Investment System is a just a mechanical strategy. There is no subjective stage analysis or ambiguity regarding entries and exits and, aside from deciding whether or not to actually participate in the stock market in the first place, all other decisions are directed by the System. Because this is a more passive strategy for investing than the method contained in *The Next Big Investment Boom*, I think it would be more suitable for those investors who lack either the experience or the inclination to delve more deeply into the subject. I personally use the System to control approximately 20 per cent of my capital, with the balance controlled by other strategies, including the one detailed in my first book. Although the System differs somewhat from the first method I revealed, there are also a number of similarities: both require minimal time spent on analysis; both are seeking to identify and exploit long-term investment trends; and both have been extremely profitable over the years.

Where the two methods differ, and the chief reason why I personally continue to use them both, is the diversity they give to my investing. The stage analysis strategy detailed in my first book can be used on all manner of assets from property, stocks and bonds through to commodities. In contrast, however, the System works primarily on stocks and shares and in particular stock market indices. I allocate some of my investment cash to the System because it guarantees that I will participate in every major stock market bull trend regardless of whether or not I've 'discovered' or 'missed' the opportunity using my other methods. In essence, I can afford to concentrate my analysis in other areas because, if there is a sustained long-term bull market in stocks, I know the System is going to catch it for me.

Sceptics and critics may wonder, 'Why would this guy give away such a goldmine for the cover price of a book?' 'Why does he not keep his methods a secret and use them to make a fortune or manage hundreds of millions of client money and earn a fortune in fees?' Well, my books might feel like 'too good to be true' purchases, but don't be put off; let me explain my motives.

As some of you may be aware, I had been a very successful hedge fund manager until I 'retired' in 1996 aged 33. When I decided to retire from public fund management it was for a specific reason, 'life balance'. Thanks to my trading and investing and the success of my fund management business, I was in a fortunate position where I had achieved sufficient wealth not to need to work or run a business any more, so I didn't. I decided to close my fund management company and return all my clients' money to them. I continued to manage my own money and still do to this day, but this takes little more than an hour a week of my time, so it's hardly 'work' in the true sense of the word. My continued success in the financial markets, coupled with my existing wealth, provides me with a perfect lifestyle. I answer to nobody but myself; I go on holiday when I want, for as long as I want; if it's a sunny day and I want to play golf, go surfing, drive my car down to a country pub for lunch, visit my mares and foals at stud or do anything else that takes my fancy, then I do. As I write this book, I'm sitting on the balcony of my cabin as I, and my family, enjoy a three-week cruise around the Mediterranean. Then I'm back home for a couple of weeks before going to Devon for two weeks' surfing. A month after that, my family and I are back on the boat for another three-week cruise to the Black Sea.

If I were still running my hedge fund business, I'm sure that the majority of my clients or the regulator wouldn't be very impressed with my holiday schedule, no matter how much money I was making. Certainly, I could be even wealthier if I had continued with my business or accepted some of the generous offers to return to the industry, but at what price? I know plenty of wealthier people who have nowhere near the personal freedom that I have, and even if they delegate the majority of their work to employees, they still seem to feel an obligation and responsibility to keep showing their face or offer their leadership. I can't be bothered. Money comes, money goes, but time is a precious commodity that can't be created, bought, sold or banked, and when it's gone it's gone. Through my interest of owning and breeding racehorses, I've already known two very successful and wealthy businessmen who not only died owing to work-related stress but, whilst they were alive, hardly ever had the time to enjoy their hobby, as their work kept them too occupied to live a proper, full life. And the real sad fact is that when these men died they both had more money than they or their families could ever have spent.

On my deathbed, I will never look back and wish I had carried on 'working' beyond 33. Even the television, radio and public speaking 'work' I conduct now, including writing this and my previous book, I undertake for the challenge and the 'crack'. If I cease to enjoy any part of it, then I'll refuse any future bookings and do something else that interests and challenges me. That's how I've managed to enjoy so many different and varied activities over the last few years. And that's why I'm not keeping this or my other methods to myself, because revealing them to you doesn't adversely affect the quality of my life. Quite the opposite, I enjoy educating and teaching people and I enjoy the positive feedback I receive. From a monetary perspective, book royalties and public-speaking fees don't even scratch the surface compared to what I can attain from investing, and I only write books, speak, teach and educate because I enjoy it. No 'bull' about sharing my good fortune with others: I reveal my systems and strategies because I can.

In addition, the stock market is so vast, with hundreds of billions invested, that I don't flatter myself to think that just by revealing my own personal methods the entire world is going to adopt them. In the grand scheme of things, the stock markets of the world will undergo their bull and bear trends based upon the fundamentals rather than the fact that 'a line in the sand' identified by Mark Shipman's System has been crossed. In short, if you and thousands of other readers adopt and religiously follow the rules of the Long-Term Investment System, it will still be just a drop in the ocean compared to the capitalization of the entire stock market. If there is an effect on prices, then those readers who follow my approach may actually be more beneficial to me than harmful, as your money combined with mine will add further impetus to a price trend that is already under way.

Using a systematic approach is a great way to invest your money, and following a well-researched and profitable strategy will instil the discipline and patience required to make a success of long-term investing. The Long-Term Investment System has a long and successful performance record, and I expect that to continue regardless of the economic future. At best, it will help you to participate in strong stock market bull trends, while seeking to protect you from the very worst bear markets. Successful investing is about allocating your cash in assets that are appreciating in value, while avoiding poor or underperforming assets. The Long-Term Investment System does what it says on the label. It is a system for investing your cash for long-term gains, and it has a successful track record dating back over five decades across all manner of economic and political crises, booms and busts. It is designed to identify and exploit long-term bull market trends in stocks and shares, and this it does very well.

In summary, I operate and follow the very System contained in this book; I put my money where my mouth is, and you will come across very few financial authors who do the same.

Happy investing!

# 1
# But why bother?

If I had known that I was going to live this long, I would have taken better care of myself.

(Eubie Blake)

Here's a question for you. Would you rather be ugly now, knowing that as you get older you'll gradually become more beautiful, or would you rather be beautiful now and worry about the future when it happens? Although this scenario may be hypothetical when we consider our appearance, when the same question is posed about our financial prosperity, subconsciously or not, the vast majority are only interested in the present day. When you're young the thought of saving and investing for retirement is usually the furthest one from your mind. Clothes, cars, jewellery or a suntan make us far more attractive people than an investment in the boring old stock market. Ironically, however, the best time to begin your investing career is while you are young because the two most important elements to the long-term success of any investment are when you start (the earlier the better) and how long you maintain your investment (the longer the better). Unfortunately, though, providing for our financial future is not a high priority, and sadly most people spend more time planning the purchase of a holiday, a car or a three-piece suite than they ever do planning their financial future. They'd rather be beautiful now and worry about the future when it happens. Another reason why this may be so is that, to the public, the world of investing dominated by pinstripe suits and economics degrees seems beyond them.

Well, that's simply not true; successfully investing your hard-earned cash isn't that difficult and, if you can follow a simple strategy that forces you to invest in assets that are rising in price and to avoid assets whose values are falling, you will outperform the majority of professionals. There aren't many professions where an amateur with a small amount of sound knowledge can outperform the professionals on a consistent basis, but thankfully investing is one of them. You owe it to yourself to take control of your financial future, because nobody else will. And the next time you visit a department store, a car showroom or a travel agent or you look in the mirror, stop and think. Are you once again sacrificing your long-term well-being for just another short-term fix? How many of your long-term plans have you suspended or cancelled to satisfy short-term desires for instant gratification? A price has to be paid; you can't do both. All long-term goals require the discipline to follow a plan, whether it's dieting, fitness, career development or investing. Drug addicts and smokers shorten their life expectancy and long-term health and happiness for just a few minutes of pleasure, and unfortunately most investors are no different.

If you can be bothered to read this book and others like it and then apply the knowledge you've gleaned to develop an investment strategy for yourself and your money, you stand a very good chance of enjoying a prosperous and happy financial future. Alternatively, you can opt to place your cash under the control of others and they can invest it on your behalf. But if you do…

# 2

# Be careful who you trust

A deluge of complaints about the mis-selling of financial products is forcing the Financial Ombudsman Service to recruit an extra 100 staff – a 16 per cent increase in its workforce. The independent appeals service for disgruntled bank and insurance customers has seen its workload increase by more than 40 per cent since April. This follows big rises over the previous two years.

*(Financial Mail on Sunday*, 14 September 2003)

The first place the public normally consider when deciding upon where to invest their hard-earned cash is with the professionals of the financial services industry. While it's important that you should safeguard your financial future, if you were considering placing your money with a professional fund manager, following the advice of a broker, stock analyst or financial adviser or even consulting your bank manager, think again. Although it is not my intention to tar everyone with the same brush and there are many competent professionals in the business, the purpose of this chapter is to make you less trusting of any particular individual or company until they can demonstrate to you that they are worthy of managing your money. I want to remove the general assumption that, if someone is a 'professional' in the world of finance, then they are automatically considered to be competent and trustworthy. In my opinion, some are about as much use as a chocolate fireguard!

# Fund managers

Over the last twenty years, only six active managers have on average managed to beat their benchmark index. Warren Buffett, the world's most famous investor, admitted last week that index trackers beat most fund managers over the long term.

(*Sunday Times*, 13 May 2007)

The above quote will probably shock you, but it's a sad fact that the vast majority of fund managers cannot even beat their respective stock market index. So, given such poor returns, why does the general public still use them? I think it's down to the assumption that because fund managers earn their living from managing other people's money they are actually good at it. Unfortunately this is usually the wrong conclusion, and market commentaries in the media do not always help because the explanations they give to describe market price action often leave the public with a false impression. For example, when a market has retraced, the action will typically be described as 'profit taking', leaving the impression that the professionals have all bought at lower levels and are now cashing in their 'chips' for a profit. Oh, if only this were true. There are many reasons why the majority of fund managers fail, which we will review later in the book, but in many cases the sole explanation for their poor performance is simply that they're just not as good at their job as the public thinks they are. To illustrate this, in an experiment recently reported in the British press, a five-year-old girl beat both stock market and financial experts by randomly picking shares. She took part in the experiment the previous year to compare different ways of predicting the movement of the market. She was pitted against two financial professionals and all three invested a virtual £5,000 in a fantasy portfolio during National Science Week. The little girl picked her stocks at random, and at the time her portfolio performed the best over one week. Then she won again over 12 months, with her portfolio being the only one that gained in value. It was up 5.8 per cent, while one expert's portfolio fell 6.2 per cent in value and the other lost a massive 46.2 per cent!

Not all fund managers are bad, but the challenge is to find the good ones, and a number of key criteria have to be met before you should consider investing. Aside from the level of management fees charged and the bid–offer spread for buying into and selling out of a fund, your main consideration has to be the quality of performance of the fund managers. How long have they managed the fund? What has been their record over one year, two years, five years or 10 years? Do they disclose whether they invest their own money in the product? Conducting this research can seem quite a daunting task but it is essential work if you want to avoid incompetent fund managers and their poorly performing products.

# Brokers/analysts

These individuals spend their time studying the market, reading company reports, communicating with company directors and investigating the odd market rumour. Their 'brief' is to ascertain the necessary information required to identify good investment opportunities for their clients, namely you, to invest in. However, a major worry with brokers/analysts is that they may often have a hidden agenda. The brokerage company that employs them may hold shares in some of the companies they research and recommend to investors as clients, and this could potentially be a conflict of interest.

Enron is just one high-profile corporation whose share price collapsed, and during the last 12 months of Enron's colossal stock drop, from a high of more than $80 per share to a low of less than $1 per share, investors lost more than $50 billion! At the very same time that stockholders were getting slaughtered, more than 50, yes 50, major brokerage firms were issuing either 'buy' or 'strong buy' recommendations for Enron shares, and these recommendations did not change even as the stock price plummeted below one dollar per share! Why? Could it be because Enron paid millions of dollars in investment banking and underwriting fees to the very same brokerage firms that sold their stock to the public? As Enron's share price collapsed, brokers and analysts chose to protect their revenue streams rather than protecting their customers, who expected accurate and unbiased financial information. In fact, some brokers actually kept their 'strong buy' recommendations on Enron stock until late November 2001, just four days before the company's bankruptcy filing!

Unfortunately, this type of abuse is not new, as illustrated by a famous old Wall Street story that goes something like this. An out-of-town visitor was being shown the wonders of the New York financial district. When he was taken to the harbour to see the luxurious boats riding at anchor, his guide proudly announced 'Look, those are the bankers' and brokers' yachts.' To this the visitor replied 'But where are their customers' yachts?'

# Tied advisers

Because tied advisers work for a single company, they can only recommend one set of products, regardless of performance. As they are unable to offer alternative, possibly better-performing products from other companies, this creates a conflict of interest that could be severely detrimental to the health of your wealth. In short, tied advisers are salespeople. For example, many years ago I was introduced to a gentleman who had spent a short period of time employed by the direct sales force of a major investment company. He was disgusted at the way these tied advisers were misselling to the general public and told me that some of his colleagues would openly boast of earning thousands of pounds a month from unsuspecting clients. This 'sell at all cost' approach has created untold misery for many decent, trusting people. Even if the tied adviser is not as unscrupulous, he or she will still place you at a serious disadvantage by not being able to offer products from other companies that may suit your investment profile better. Also, do not be caught out if the adviser is a friend or member of the family. When these advisers begin their careers, they are normally instructed to hit friends and family first, because the selling process is considered much easier if they pick on the people closest to them.

If you regularly scan the financial press you will be aware that, in the worst cases, the misselling of investment products nearly always features a tied adviser, and unless someone you can personally trust recommends one, you deal with them at your peril!

# Independent financial advisers

Independent financial advisers (IFAs) are without a doubt in the best position to offer you advice and are definitely worthy of consideration. Because they are able to review and offer products from a wide variety of different sources, they are in a far more flexible position than the tied adviser, and if you decide to seek outside help with your personal investing, then I recommend it should be to an IFA that you turn. Your local telephone directory will detail all the IFAs in your area, and as you shouldn't be required to pay for an initial consultation you may find it useful to visit more than one and compare notes before committing to employ their services. Better still is to find someone you trust who has used an IFA and is happy with the service he or she received. Finally though, always remember that an IFA's income is generated from commissions, so you should still do your homework before parting with your cash.

# Other professionals

Investment bank Morgan Stanley has agreed to pay £30 million to settle charges over its mutual fund sales practices. Morgan was fined £1.18 million in September by the US National Association of Securities Dealers for offering improper incentives to its sales staff – including Britney Spears tickets – to push its mutual funds.

(*Daily Mail*, 18 November 2003)

The mis-selling of endowments has cost life insurers up to £700 million in fines, compensation, administration and Ombudsmen fees. Some experts estimate a final cost of up to £3 billion.

(*Mail on Sunday*, 30 March 2003)

Sadly, today the biggest threat to your financial well-being could come from your bank. You may have thought that only financial advisers receive commissions from the investment transactions that you undertake; however, the truth is that the banking profession also engages in the commissioned selling of investment products. Although banks and their employees provide a valuable service to businesses and individuals, a recent television programme changed that perception for many people, myself included. The programme placed one of their reporters undercover in a call centre of one of the major banks, and over the course of filming the undercover reporter was encouraged to sell high-commission, inappropriate and unprofitable investment products to the bank's customers. On one occasion, a member of staff was filmed trying to sell a life assurance package with no medical to a customer, knowing full well this same customer had earlier been refused a personal loan because the customer had a terminal illness! Unfortunately, it's easy to see how customers can be misled. Banks are in a respected and revered position, with generations having been brought up to regard them as a fountain of sound financial knowledge, yet some are turning their employees into nothing more than commissioned salespeople, and this is a major conflict of interest. In addition, because banks sell their own products, you also run the same risks I've already referred to with tied advisers. Therefore, you should treat any advice given by your bank with the utmost caution, and when selecting a suitable institution with which to place your money you won't go too far wrong if you take the advice of the music impresario Lol Pryor: 'The best bank to have your account with is the one where you can park your car outside!'

# 3

# How to spot the friend from the foe

Be wary of the man who urges an action in which he himself incurs no risk.

(Joaquin Setanti)

I was recently interviewed on Ireland's world-famous television programme, RTE's *The Late Late Show* (you can see this on the internet by typing www.rte.ie/tv/latelate/20070420.html), and one of the stories I recounted drew a massive response from viewers. It was about someone I had met who had been an unsuccessful double-glazing salesperson but had miraculously turned his sales career around by selling financial products instead. This was despite the fact that the individual concerned had received just minimal training before switching from windows to finance. He credited his success to how people reacted to the different products he was selling. He said that, in his previous career, potential customers would always ask lots of questions before committing to buy or would refuse to buy anything until they had checked out quotes from other double-glazing companies. Yet now he was selling financial products, nobody asked any questions before they bought and they didn't shop around for other financial products either. As he told me, 'I resurrected my career by keeping the pinstripe suit but changing the products I sold from windows to finance. And the mad thing is, I still know more about double glazing than I do about investing!'

It's an unfortunate state of affairs when people spend more time and effort over the selection of a window than their financial future. Assuming you are prepared to exercise some effort, how is it possible to detect whether the advice or service you are receiving is competent, honest and genuine?

Firstly, always beware of cold calls. If you receive an unsolicited telephone call from a person or company you do not know, the chances are you could become the victim of a cold call. Unfortunately, there has recently been an increase in such unsolicited calls, primarily from overseas (in particular Spain and the United States), and I've been made aware of two innocent people who've already parted with up to £10,000 each only to find out their money has disappeared. Unscrupulous financial salespeople obtain your name and telephone number from lists, and typically the person who calls you is operating from a script. These scripts have a uniform introduction, and a pat, standard response for almost any objection that you may offer. If the salesperson calling you seems to have a ready answer for any question or objection that you may offer or tries to instil in you a sense of urgency, the chances are that he or she is using a script, and the best remedy, before you and your money are quickly parted, is to hang up the telephone.

Secondly, before investing any of your own money you should fully understand what you are investing in, and if you do not understand how the investment product you are being sold works, do not buy it. Financial salespeople exploit the ignorance of the investing public, and the best antidote when dealing with these people is to remember the words of Donald Trelford, 'If you don't understand a complicated financial idea it does not necessarily follow that you're stupid. The notion itself may be fundamentally flawed.'

Thirdly, clarify before you invest whether the salesperson recommending the financial product has invested any of his or her money in the same product. This is a due diligence question used by many of the world's richest investors before they make their decisions on where to invest their multimillion-pound portfolios, and I suggest that you adopt it too. If advisers cannot prove they have invested their own money in the product they are trying to sell you, the odds favour that you are about to be sold an overpriced and underperforming investment. Every day, investors are lured into parting with their hard-earned cash to participate in schemes that the salesperson would personally avoid like the plague. It doesn't make sense to enter a car dealership and buy a car from a salesperson who owns and drives a different make, and the same applies to investment products.

It is also important to remember that in every financial transaction everyone in the chain will be getting paid one way or the other. Commission-based income can act like a drug to some salespeople, who soon become addicted, and like all addicts they will often do anything to feed their habit. Selling the most rewarding investment product to them by way of the commission earned, without any consideration of the customer in terms of the product's actual performance, is gross misconduct. When investing in any financial product, you owe it to yourself to find out exactly who is benefiting from your investment and by how much.

Here's one tactic you could consider when selecting financial advice. As financial salespeople will typically ask you a lot of personal questions about your financial state of affairs, I favour flipping the questioning process around and asking them a few, which may help you identify and avoid the rogues. Remember the story at the beginning of this chapter about the double-glazing salesman?

- *Question 1:* How much are they personally worth? Would you take financial advice from a poor person?!
- *Question 2:* Where have they invested their own money? This is the most important question to ask. It follows the reasoning of the previous paragraphs in that you should never put your own money into any investment that the advisers or salespeople themselves would not or do not participate in.
- *Question 3:* What was their career before becoming financial advisers or salespeople? Hopefully they will have had some experience in finance; otherwise this could be a warning sign. That said, I actually think it's more important how they react to this question rather than what they say. If they appear angry at your enquiry into their past, I would be very wary. On the other hand, regardless of their previous career, if they seem happy to talk this usually means they are very comfortable with them-selves and confident in their ability to perform for you.

- *Question 4:* How long have they been in the financial services business? As in any profession, longevity is usually a sign of success. The longer they have been in business, the greater the probability that they are good at their job. Do not gamble your money on the advice of an unproven novice. It is better to be safe than sorry. After all, it's not their money they lose if they are wrong; it's yours!
- *Question 5:* How long has their most loyal customer been using their services? As with the previous question, longevity is usually a sign of success. If they have been in business many years and have clients who have remained loyal throughout, then this is usually an indication that they are competent.
- *Question 6:* Do they have any clients who would be happy to vouch for their integrity and the profitability of the investment advice they have provided? Customer referrals are extremely helpful, and if provided, always check them out.

It is no bad thing to put these people 'on the spot'; if they are competent and successful, their answers should give you comfort in following their recommendations. However, if they seem on edge during the questioning or some of their answers don't seem convincing enough, lose them quickly before they start losing your money.

Perhaps the clearest warning that you could be receiving bad advice is if you are asked to consider a 'low-risk' investment that has produced fantastic performance returns over a short period of time. The 'hot' thing could have made over 100 per cent during the last 12 months, but while this sounds exciting, always remember that if an investment sounds too good to be true it usually is! This is because the relationship between risk and reward is one that cannot be broken. As a rough guide, any investment that has posted a big return over a short period of time will have taken an equally big risk, got lucky or both!

High Short-Term Performance Record = Luck and/or High Risk

That said, you can only apply this logic to short-term performance numbers of less than a couple of years because a longer-term record benefits from compounding, which can enable low-risk investments to post big returns over the long term. Just to complicate things further, a low return does not necessarily mean low risk; it might just be that the investment is no good.

Despite my concerns about the quality of some financial advice offered to the public, I want to state that I believe

> not all institutions, fund managers and financial advisers are bad, but...

if you are going to trust someone else with your money, do your homework and understand what you are investing in and who you are investing with. And if you have any reservations and you cannot get a satisfactory answer, you shouldn't invest your money. As our good friend Socrates once said, 'the only evil is ignorance'.

# 4

# You can beat the professionals

Thankfully there is an alternative to blindly turning your cash over to other people, and considering the fact that the performance record of the majority of professionals isn't very good, you will soon see why I believe it is possible for a complete novice to outperform the pinstripe brigade over the long term. As an individual investor you have a number of serious advantages over the professional fund manager, and with the help of a simple and robust system such as the one detailed in this book, you can comfortably outperform the vast majority of actively managed investment funds.

To be fair to some fund managers, they are subject to a number of restrictions that govern how they can manage money, and in many cases this can affect their long-term performance. I know how this feels, because when I first traded in the City and was told to specialize in sterling interest rate products I had the same problem. When the markets had momentum, things were fine and I made money, but when they went quiet, making a profit was like getting blood from a stone and because I wasn't permitted to trade other asset classes or markets my hands were tied and my performance handicapped.

Specialization is a double-edged sword for many fund managers because the performance of the particular stock market sector or country they have to cover will have a profound effect on their own returns. For instance, during the dotcom boom of the late 1990s, any manager or investment fund specializing in technology stocks should have had a fantastic performance. However, when the technology bubble burst their performance returns typically suffered the same fate. Because they were managing a technology fund, the fund managers had to invest in tech stocks and, unfortunately, in a bear market even the share prices of the good companies go down. The manager can always sell his or her holdings and 'go to cash' (all money is removed from stocks and placed on deposit), but very few do and many aren't allowed to lower their stock market exposure below a certain percentage, which means they have to maintain holding positions despite a market in free fall.

Country- or continent-specific fund managers have exactly the same problem, and in the late 1980s managers specializing in Japanese stocks became the 'darlings' of their industry as the Japanese stock market climbed several hundred per cent in the space of just a few years. However, when this market reversed and headed into a long and vicious bear trend, these heroes and their high-performing funds suddenly became the villains. Fund managers specializing in Japanese stocks cannot liquidate and reinvest in European or US shares because that goes against the very essence of the product they are managing.

Many years ago when I ran my own hedge fund management company, I learnt that successful fund management was essentially about marketing. It's no different today, and fund management companies are continually repackaging old products, introducing new ones or window-dressing their performance numbers to appeal to whatever the general investing public currently desires. The big fund management companies spend fortunes advertising 'new' financial products capitalizing on the current vogue. Today it might be funds investing in the Asian emerging markets, with a heavy emphasis on China and India, while tomorrow it could be commodity-based funds. Successful fund management is about successful marketing, and in many cases overall performance comes a very poor second. No matter how badly a fund is currently performing, good marketing can always cover up the cracks. If the last two years' performance of a particular fund hasn't been very strong, then the fund management company will either not market that fund at all or use performance periods that cover longer time frames such as 10 or 15 years until the returns look attractive to investors. Fund management companies are in the business of selling their products, nothing more and nothing less. If performance is poor, they will create new products or dress up the returns of their existing funds to show them in a better light.

That's how the professionals cope with poorly performing stock market sector-specific, country-specific or global returns, but as a private investor you have much more freedom. You can actually switch your money out of the bad and into the good. If Japan or tech stocks perform well, then invest in them; however, if they perform badly you can drop them and look for opportunities elsewhere. If there appear to be no good investment options at that moment in time, as a private investor you are free to place all of your money in a deposit account to earn interest until conditions improve and the next signal to invest is generated.

To guide you through such a process all you need is a simple tried-and-tested method that will signal when you need to invest in the stock market and when not to, and I believe the approach detailed in this book will do that job for you. Investment management is one of the few professions on the planet where a complete amateur, with just a little guidance, can outperform the professional, but don't just take my word for it. This is what Peter Lynch, one of the leading fund managers in the world, with billions of dollars under his control, had to say about the subject in his book *One Up on Wall Street*:

> Twenty years in this business convinces me that any normal person using the customary three percent of the brain can pick stocks just as well, if not better, than the average Wall Street expert. I know you don't expect the plastic surgeon to advise you to do your own facelift, nor the plumber to tell you to install your own hot water tank, nor the hairdresser to recommend that you trim your own bangs, but this isn't surgery or plumbing or hairdressing. This is investing, where the smart money isn't so smart, and the dumb money isn't really as dumb as it thinks.

Over the last few years, I've worked with a number of 'amateur' investors who are now enjoying healthy returns from their investments just by following easy-to-use systematic strategies. In addition, letters and e-mails from readers of my first book provide further evidence that if you have the discipline to follow an approach that forces you to invest in assets that are rising in price and liquidate those that are falling in value, you can make impressive returns. Reading certain financial books literally changed my life and transformed me from a 'punting' trader at a City bank to the CEO of one of the fastest-growing hedge fund businesses in the world (and I owned the company 100 per cent) in the space of three years. I re-educated myself with books that cost no more than the price of a meal at a decent restaurant. If you can adopt a positive mental attitude and have faith in your ability to follow the rules of a successful system, then you can take on the professionals and beat them.

# 5

# But...

Before I go any further, I think this is a good point in the book to identify and examine some of the main reasons why most private investors fail. If you recognize any of the following traits in yourself or your approach to investing, now is a good time to re-evaluate your methods of operation. When it comes to investing your money in the markets, there are a number of pitfalls, and I hope that by identifying the most common and important ones it will help you not to repeat them. The main reason why I believe a systematic approach to investing outperforms the majority of fund managers, financial advisers, traders and investors is that such an approach minimizes the risk of bad habits creeping in. In the world of sport, and particularly in the highly technical game of golf, it's been mentioned on numerous occasions that perfection doesn't exist and the best players are those who make the fewest mistakes. The same is also very true of investing in the markets; perfection doesn't exist and the best investors are the ones who usually make the fewest mistakes. Bad habits lead to mistakes, which, in turn, create poor performance.

Whether you are a professional or new to investing, the following errors of judgement and psychological faults are equally applicable, and if you recognize any in yourself, now is as good a time as any to change your ways. This list is not definitive; nor is it in any particular order of importance because, either individually or collectively, each one has the power to sabotage your investing.

# A failure to set goals

If you aim at nothing, that's what you'll hit.

(Anon)

One of the most important elements to success when undertaking any endeavour is to set yourself goals. It's what separates the truly successful from the rest. Whether it's a diet, a sport, personal development, business management, or trading and investing, setting clearly defined goals most definitely increases your chances of long-term success. When you identify goals it helps you to crystallize what you want and set out a plan for attainment.

However, to be effective the targets you set yourself need to be realistic and achievable if the strategy is to work. Setting yourself goals that you have no realistic hope of achieving will only result in disappointment. Certainly, we'd all like to double our money every month or start with £1,000 and be a millionaire by the end of the year, but in all honesty such targets are meaningless because setting goals only works if the goals are realistically achievable. The real beauty of well-planned goals is they keep you focused on where you want to be and how you're going to get there. And they work; but you don't just have to take my word for it. In a famous and often-quoted experiment conducted at Yale University in 1953, a group of graduates were asked if they had ever written or thought of specific goals in their life. Only 3 per cent of the group responded that they had clear, written goals. In 1973, the entire group was revisited and, 20 years on, the 3 per cent who had used goals to focus their lives and careers had accumulated more wealth than the other 97 per cent combined. As with most things in life, there are no guarantees, but you can do a lot to put the odds of success in your favour, and I believe nowhere is this more apparent than when you're investing your own cash. Setting out what you want to achieve works.

However, when you set yourself targets, there are a number of important considerations to make, and in his best-selling book *Forecasting Financial Markets* (see 'Further reading'), Tony Plummer sets out the following practical requirements for effective goal setting:

in order to establish a goal that will be effective for you:

■ It must be stated in the positive rather than in the negative. It is important to be precise about exactly what is required, rather than merely eliminate undesirable conditions. The subconscious probably already knows what you don't want anyway, which is why it keeps projecting negative emotions at you.

■ It must be ecological – in the sense of being consistent with your relationships with other people, with your environment and, indeed, with your beliefs about life. In other words, it must fit completely and naturally into your life and preserve balance.

■ It must be stated in terms of a relevant context. Your subconscious will need to know exactly when, where and with whom you want the outcome. The realization of the goal must be placed within an effective time frame. Obviously a goal that is to be realized within the space of a few months is going to generate more energy than one that is to be realized within an ill-defined number of years. However, the time period must be practical. Doubling your income in two years is a more practical objective than doubling it within one month.

■ It must be defined in terms of a sensory experience. It is important that you know what it will be like to have the outcome. Hence, you should be able to visualize what it will be like to have the outcome. You should be able to see, hear and feel it in as much detail as you can.

■ It must be within your power to initiate and maintain the resources necessary to produce the outcome. If you are unable to produce the resources or effect the necessary changes in the environment, then the project will not get off the ground. It would, for example, not be practical to trade the market without sufficient capital.

Although Plummer's advice may seem a little 'new age' and heavy going to some of you, bear with him and me. Reread his recommendations until you fully understand what's required when you set yourself a goal, and be wary of dismissing such advice, because it will only handicap you when it comes to investing your money. In essence, identifying strong, well-founded and realistic personal targets is the key to developing a plan of action, and if you want to be a successful investor you're going to need a plan.

# A failure to plan

With a plan, you can get back on course when you go astray. But without a plan, you can't even know you're off course.

(Paul Merriman)

The mantra 'A failure to plan is a plan for failure' is used in many fields of endeavour, particularly in the military, but nowhere is it more accurate than when applied to speculating in the markets.

Planning is an essential ingredient for a profitable career in investing yet probably the most overlooked aspect. Ironically, people are planners by nature. For example, when we go on holiday we book time off work; arrange flights or transport; book accommodation; and pack our luggage according to the climate of the holiday destination. And it's not just holidays: people spend considerable amounts of their time on the purchase of a three-piece suite, car and other 'important' items. Yet when it comes to budgeting, controlling and/or investing their money, comparatively little time is devoted. It's no wonder the majority always have money problems.

Another useful saying I often use in presentations is: 'You get more of what you focus on.' What does this mean? Well, if you spend most of your thinking time dreaming about luxuries such as iPods, CDs, TVs, furniture or holidays, then that's your focus and that's what you will end up with. I recently watched a television programme that attempted to help people who were in a poor financial position through running up debts on credit cards. The first 'contestant' had managed to run up credit card debts of £75,000, purchasing anything and everything. Her job paid her little more than £14,000 a year, so this lady was in considerable financial trouble. Disregarding how she was allowed to run up such huge debts by the banks and credit card companies, which in itself is another subject and book altogether, I was interested to see exactly what she had been buying: clothes and shoes. Tens of thousands of pounds' worth of shoes, most of which were still in their boxes, unused, and similarly large amounts of designer clothing, also unused. The second individual we were introduced to was a lorry driver who had run up considerable debts purchasing gadgets, anything from laptop computers through to flat-screen televisions and mobile phones. He also had four iPods, *four,* each one being the latest version at the time he purchased it, but hardly a sensible strategy if you've only got one pair of ears. Now, you may argue that the subjects of this programme were extreme cases and only used because they make good television, and to a degree you would be right, but they are prime examples of 'You get what you focus on.' In both cases, in addition to their spending, the individuals bought magazines about the objects of their desires. The lady read fashion magazines and the lorry driver read gadget magazines. The power of focus cannot be underestimated.

On a more positive note, if you were to focus some of your 'free-thinking' time on your finances, there's a strong chance that your effort would bring reward. This book isn't about reducing debt or saving money on purchases: I'll leave that to other authors like Alvin Hall and Martin Lewis. Its focus is about making money from investing. And that's what you will need to focus on if you want to be successful from participating in the markets. I've already discussed the setting of clearly defined and achievable goals, and the natural result of this is to then develop a plan or strategy to achieve those goals. You owe it to yourself to sit down and write a plan of how much money you need or have got to invest, when and where you're going to invest it, and what investment strategy or system you're going to apply. If you're in control of investing your own cash, you must avoid the scatter-gun haphazard approach that the majority of people use. Basing your investing on broker tips, magazine recommendations, something a mate told you down the pub or gut feel will not change your financial future for the better, yet unfortunately this is how most people handle their money.

In 1999, *Fortune* magazine published an article that stated that people who had written plans for controlling their investments had, on average, five times more money during retirement than those without any such strategy. Of course, the mere act of planning your investing doesn't instantly guarantee success, but it does help to keep you focused on the right path. Effective financial planning should involve taking stock of where you are at the moment and the level of financial stability you either have or don't have, calculating how much money you have available to invest, establishing your appetite for risk, and setting realistic goals for the next 10, 20 or 30 years and a strategy that will guide your investment decisions along the way. If you feel such a task is too daunting, a competent independent financial adviser should be able to assist you. One thing you should remember, though, is not to undertake any investment or investment strategy until you have a plan.

# Assumption

> Assumption is the mother of all f**k-ups!
>
> (From the film *Lock, Stock and Two Smoking Barrels*)

No apologies for the crude language content in the above quote because I don't want you to forget it or the problems assumption causes when investing in the markets. An investor should never 'assume', and many a fortune has been lost because people wrongly assumed that:

■ they knew something the rest of the market didn't;
■ they were right and the market was wrong;
■ a market couldn't move in a certain direction;
■ the share price(s) couldn't fall below a particular level;
■ a company couldn't be as bad as the fundamentals suggested;

and so on.

If you ever find yourself rationalizing a strategy or the holding of an investment position with an assumption that a certain scenario can't or shouldn't happen, be very afraid, because every now and again the markets have a nasty habit of doing the exact opposite of what people expect them to do. Never assume anything, and always prepare for the fact that you or your strategy may, on this occasion, be wrong. Essentially if you 'assume' anything it can lead to complacency or overconfidence, which in turn could result in taking too big a risk. Back in September 1929 or at the beginning of January 1973, the end of September 1987 or the end of 1999, the majority of investors 'assumed' that the stock market was a one-way bet and it could do nothing but go up. These assumptions were obviously wrong, and many were bankrupted because they never factored into their investing or trading the fact that the markets might eventually stop moving higher and reverse.

Another dangerous but common assumption many make is to assume they are better at speculating in the markets than they actually are. In the above-mentioned periods of history, investors who were lucky enough to be involved in the sharply rising markets began to 'assume' that their profits were a direct result of their 'expertise' and 'skill' rather than the fact that they were just fortunate enough to be in the right place at the right time. The industry typically labels such participants as having experienced a 'bull market for brains' delusion. And as these investors become ever more complacent, they disregard risk and aggressively increase their commitments when in truth they are setting themselves up for a nasty shock at some point in the future. The typical assumption that tends to appear during such periods is that 'this time around things are different'. Unfortunately this is rarely, if ever, the case. There will always be people who become seduced by 'easy' profits, and once they start to assume they have become experts it's just a question of time before they are wiped out.

The best antidote to 'assumption' is to be humble. Although I've earned my living from trading and investing in the markets over the last 20 years and I have confidence in my ability and that of the strategies I use, I still remain humble and aware that on any occasion my analysis or my investment positions could be wrong. The market price is never wrong or right — it's just the market price – and I never make assumptions about the current or future direction of prices. My core investing philosophy is to accept the best but always to be prepared for the worst.

# Procrastination

This is a common life problem for many people and a particularly negative quality if you're an investor. No matter what the endeavour may be, many people can 'talk the talk' but very few can 'walk the walk', and the major difference between successful individuals and the rest of society is not that they are of a higher intelligence or possess God-given skills or luck; it's typically down to the fact that they're 'doers' as opposed to talkers. Unfortunately, when the majority of people have a good idea, that's where it stays – in their head. Have you ever met someone who had an investment or business idea that sounded like a great money-making opportunity, but when you met them again a few days or weeks later and enquired how they were progressing, you got the response 'Oh, I haven't got round to doing anything about it yet'? In short, procrastination will lead to missed opportunities; whether such behaviour is born out of a lack of confidence, a fear of being wrong, a fear of losing money or just plain laziness, it is dangerous to your wealth.

Dealing specifically with investing, procrastination causes one of two unprofitable outcomes. Firstly, you will miss opportunities because you hesitated to act when a signal or instruction to invest was generated, and secondly, you hesitate to liquidate an investment, again not acting upon a signal or instruction, which now leaves you exposed to further losses if the investment in question continues to go down in value. Avoid procrastinating. Where is the logic in using a sound investment strategy if you then fail to act upon the signals it generates?

Losers procrastinate; winners don't.

# Requiring perfection

It is incredible how rich you can get by not being perfect.

(Larry Hite)

Although the above quote is one I often include in my presentations and also appears in my first book, I think it deserves its place in this book as well. Larry Hite is a 'market wizard' and a founder of one of the largest hedge fund management companies in the world. His opinion deserves respect.

Whenever I discuss my occupation with a new acquaintance at a dinner party or other social gathering, they always seem to have the misconception that professional traders or investors go through their careers just opening positions, watching profits accumulate and then banking them before moving on to the next guaranteed certainty. In addition, people usually think that to be successful in this business you need to have a foolproof system or 'inside information' and dismiss my claims that I often have losing positions and that the real key to my success is actually down to the boring attributes of patience and discipline. Also, through my speaking engagements I meet many people who want to invest or trade their money but say they are waiting to discover the perfect system or approach. Typically such individuals have tried every technical indicator, purchased and read all the books, attended numerous seminars, and bought many publicly advertised systems, as well as researching and developing their own, but they 'haven't found anything fool-proof enough' to commit their money to. They are searching for perfection.

Well, I'm sorry to disappoint, but unfortunately such perfection doesn't exist. There is no Holy Grail. However, don't be disappointed for too long, because the good news is you don't need a perfect strategy to make a fortune from investing. What really sets successful investors apart is not that they don't have losing positions or periods of poor performance; it's how they react and respond to such losses that counts. And if there is such a thing as the 'Holy Grail of Investing', then I believe it involves managing the inevitable losses whilst maximizing profits: that's the edge of a successful investor.

Forget about searching for perfection when it comes to investing, because I'm afraid it doesn't exist, and anyone who sells you a book, product or seminar claiming otherwise is a liar.

## Trying to buy the lows and sell the highs

*The most intelligent way to begin managing money is to confess you don't have a clue where the markets are going.*

(Hugh Johnson)

Another one of the popular misconceptions I come across about how professional investors operate is that we have some sixth sense about the direction of a market and an ability to predict price levels where the market will reach a top or a bottom. This view is further re-inforced by unscrupulous system sellers who advertise their products in publications and on the internet with claims such as

'Identifies market highs and lows months in advance', 'Predicted the bottom of the bear market', 'Sold the all-time high', etc.

Not only is it not possible to consistently identify such turning points, because the market cannot be analysed that accurately, but it also isn't necessary. I, and many professionals like me, have made a very satisfactory living by never selling the high or buying the low and, on many occasions, not even getting close to such price levels. Profitable investing is the result of far more boring criteria such as discipline, patience and operating a sound, well-researched strategy. Investors who become preoccupied with attempts to pick tops and bottoms in market cycles usually not only end up missing strong market trends but often find themselves positioned the wrong way round, and I would hazard a guess that more money is lost and more traders and investors go broke trying to pick tops and bottoms than with any other speculative tactic. If you have ever been fortunate enough to sell a market cycle high or buy a low, accept that you were just lucky, because continuing to repeat such a feat is the quickest route to the poorhouse.

# Allowing your emotions to control your investment decisions

A Native American grandfather talking to his young grandson tells the boy that he has two wolves inside him struggling with each other. The first is the wolf of peace, love and kindness. The other wolf is fear, greed and hatred. 'Which wolf will win, grandfather?' asks the young boy. 'Whichever one I feed' is the reply.

(A Native American proverb)

One particularly important ingredient in the make-up of successful traders and investors is the control they have over their emotions. I classify this attribute as EQ (emotional intelligence) as opposed to IQ, which is the usual measurement of intelligence. I believe that emotional intelligence or mental strength, call it what you will, is the key quality required to be a successful speculator, and perhaps this explains why so many obviously intellectually intelligent (high IQ) people fail when it comes to participating in the markets. Typically when referring to how emotions influence and affect investors, the twin demons of 'fear' and 'greed' are mentioned, and if you break down most of the key drivers to our decision making it does indeed come down to these emotions:

- the *fear* of losing our money, the fear of not making enough money, the fear of making the wrong investment, and the fear of failure;
- the *greed* of trying to make too much money too quickly (which typically involves high risk), the greed of wishing we'd invested even more in a winning position than we have, and the greed that leads to an investor abandoning a sound strategy just because it has hit a period of poor performance.

If you allow such emotions to gain the upper hand, it will lead to an unhealthy focus on returns at the expense of ignoring the risks. If you do not control your emotions, you will not make a success of investing, no matter how 'clever' you are!

In summary, these are just some of the main faults, mistakes and misconceptions that can sabotage your investing and result in you underachieving your financial and personal goals. Thankfully, there is an alternative, and just by reading this chapter you should have already been able to identify where you may have been going wrong in the past. In addition, I've included in this book a tried-and-tested strategy for exploiting long-term bull market trends in stocks and shares. I can personally vouch for the profitability of the strategy from both historical testing on decades of stock market history and actual real-time application investing my own cash. The System is not ambiguous; it provides clear-cut, easily identifiable buy and sell signals, and if you strictly follow the rules as shown you will end up with exactly the same positions as me. It doesn't matter whether you are a complete novice or a seasoned professional; the discipline of following such a methodology will provide you with the same results regardless of your prior market experience or lack of it. As the saying goes, 'The proof of the pudding is in the eating', and over the years, as well as experiencing my own success, I've met numerous investors, both professional and amateur, who've benefited from using a systematic approach to speculating in the markets. Now you also have that opportunity.

# 6

# Systematic investing

Although not all of my own strategies for investing and trading revolve around the use of systems, I believe that, whether you are a newcomer or already have some market experience, you will definitely benefit from understanding how an investment system works and the disciplines it forces upon you. I am not suggesting that systematic investing is your only option, nor is it a get-rich-quick solution, but, as I will cover in the next few chapters, it does provide an investor, and particularly a novice, with a formula that has proven itself profitable over many years. And because a system is nothing more than a tool for investing in the stock market, it has many advantages over a human trying to make the same decisions. Systems never suffer from peer pressure or being opinionated, egotistic, complacent, vengeful, upset, angry, jealous, overconfident or in denial; they are never fooled by political, corporate, media or broker/analyst spin. However, humans often are!

Whilst running my hedge fund management business back in the 1990s, I vividly remember a conversation I had with one of my wealthiest clients, a very well-known and successful investor in his own right, about the subject of emotional pressure. My client said that he never invested money with any discretionary fund manager who was going through a divorce, about to become a parent or in the process of moving house. He explained that past experiences had taught him that strong outside distractions such as these always had a negative impact on the performance of a manager. However, in contrast to an individual making discretionary decisions, an investment system concentrates on just one thing, the market.

I believe the key to long-term success lies in using a strategy that contains just a few robust rules that have been proven to stand the test of time.

So where's my proof?

Well, in addition to the profitable performance of my own approaches, let me introduce you to Marty Zweig, a highly respected fund manager and the author of a book on stock market systems called *Winning on Wall Street* (see 'Further reading'). Originally published back in 1986, Marty's book shows how an investor can consistently outperform the market and the majority of professional fund managers from just a few minutes' work each week. Essentially his approaches combine both simple monetary and price momentum indicators into a 'super model' that seeks to maximize returns whilst minimizing risk.

To prove that Marty Zweig and his strategies aren't just a one-off, Michael O'Higgins, another highly successful investment manager, published his own ingenious strategy in the book *Beating the Dow* (see 'Further reading'). The book immediately became a best-seller, and O'Higgins's system spawned a veritable industry, including websites, mutual funds and over $20 billion worth of investments. His approach essentially involves an annual review of the performance of the 30 stocks that make up the Dow Jones Industrial Average. The process takes no more than a few minutes each year to operate and involves selecting a short list of high-dividend-yielding, low-priced stocks to be held for the next 12 months, whereupon you repeat the selection process for the coming year. Despite its simplicity and the almost complete lack of effort required to operate the system, O'Higgins's 'Dogs of the Dow', to use its popular name, has an impressive long-term performance record. However, many still refuse to accept that there is a substitute for hard work and burning the midnight oil poring over hundreds of company reports. As O'Higgins recently wrote, 'I expected the simplicity of the strategy would meet with scepticism in a financial community addicted to the notion that anything as important as managing money had to be complicated.'

The success of O'Higgins's system has spawned a number of other similar approaches, one of the most popular being 'the Foolish Four', which comes from the highly respected and very successful Motley

Fool website: www.fool.com. This method also focuses upon high-yielding stocks, is operated just once a year (typically in late December) and takes just a few minutes to operate. And again it has a long-term track record that most professional fund managers can only dream about.

In addition, the British newspaper *Mail on Sunday* has operated another successful simple system. Constructed and working in a similar way to O'Higgins's method, the *Mail on Sunday*'s version focuses on the British stock market and is aptly titled 'the Dogs of the Footsie [FTSE]'. Every quarter, the newspaper reviews and adjusts the stockholdings of the 'Dogs' portfolio, and since it began operating the strategy a few years ago the performance has been outstanding:

> Look how our portfolio has performed since its launch in 2001. If you had invested £10,000 and followed our advice every step of the way, your investments would be now worth £17,493, a gain of almost 75% based on share prices late last week. Over the same period, the Footsie (FTSF 100 Index) has risen about 4%; an investment of £10,000 would be worth £10,400. No investment system is foolproof, but the Dogs approach continues to serve us well. We are happy to stick with it.
>
> (*Mail on Sunday*, July 2006)

These results are fantastic, especially compared to the performance of the fund management industry, hedge and traditional, over the same period. All again for just a few minutes' effort.

It is no coincidence that the performance of these methods and that of my very own Long-Term Investment System has been so profitable, way more profitable than many activities within the general investing community. I believe that the success of such strategies proves beyond doubt that profitable investing is not about working hard but working smart. There aren't many professions or endeavours in life where such little effort can achieve such outstanding returns, but investing in the markets is one of them. There is no need for you to be clever and to attempt to reinvent the wheel; you just need to find out what works for you, which is all I've done.

# 7

# The benefits of evaluating a system

Systems can be a great tool for an investor. They impart discipline and focus your cash into assets that have historically been proven to outperform over the long run. How do I know this? Because one of the most outstanding attributes of using a systematic approach is the ability to test its performance on decades of historical data and numerous market cycles. Not only will such research illustrate whether or not the system is profitable, but it will also indicate under what market conditions it performs the best and the worst. This information is enormously useful, because once you know the empirical characteristics of a strategy you will have a fair idea how it will react if the markets enter a similar period again. Knowing in advance just how a strategy will perform given different market conditions helps an investor to prepare for and cope with the psychological pressures that can occur when you hit a period of low or flat performance.

For example, if you adopt a trend-following strategy and the markets aren't trending, you know that you will not make any decent returns at that moment in time; however, you also know that, when the markets once again begin to trend, as they always eventually do, then you will enjoy strong profits. Compare this on the other hand to investing your cash in a managed fund or product controlled by a manager or team of managers. If you invested your money now with a fund manager who has only been in the job for a few years, you have no idea how the fund manager will perform if market trends change because the manager may not have experienced such conditions before. This is a very real risk, especially when you consider that most managers of hedge funds and traditional products have been in the business for just a few years at best.

In his excellent book *Fooled by Randomness* (see 'Further reading'), Nassim Nicholas Taleb recounts a personal experience where he watched a young ambitious corporate bond trader work his way up through the ranks to become the 'darling' of the company. This trader's outstanding performance was attributed at the time to his expertise and 'feel' for high-yield corporate bonds and, according to Taleb, this gentleman's net worth went from nothing to over $15 million in the space of a few years, purely as a result of the bonuses his employers paid him. As his performance numbers continued to grow, so the company gave him ever-larger amounts to manage until, in the summer of 1998, the trend in high-yield bonds turned. At the time this didn't worry the 'gifted' trader because, throughout his short career, every time the bond market had fallen he had simply increased his positions and made even greater profits when the market finally resumed its trend. This time, however, prices didn't recover; the bull market had finished. Over the previous seven years, this trader had made his employers around $250 million, but in the space of just a few days he lost $600 million! Multiple years' accumulated profits gone in less than a week!

Was this 'gifted' bond trader unlucky or had he just been in the right place at the right time during a strong bull market in bond prices and experienced a 'bull market for brains' career? Unfortunately for him, his employers and their investors, it was the latter. Because he had only been in the business a comparatively short period of time, his only experience had come from participating in a bull market and he never acknowledged, accepted or probably even understood that markets can trend down as well as up in price. Such lack of experience ultimately led to his downfall.

Now compare this to using a systematic strategy where you can select any period in history, favourable or unfavourable, and test how the approach would have performed. Nowadays, one of the great advantages investors have over past generations is the personal computer. For relatively little expense, powerful machines can be purchased that, combined with excellent software packages, make it possible for anyone interested in the subject to test and validate their own or someone else's system in a matter of hours, if not minutes. Using just a few mouse clicks, you can research a strategy on decades of market data to see if it has any validity. This is a far cry from a few years ago, when I honestly had to conduct all such research by hand, using volumes of historical charts, a pencil, a pocket calculator and a very large magnifying glass! Today's software is more than capable of providing you with every important piece of information about the idea you are researching. Such feedback is enormously useful because not only will the results indicate whether the method under research is profitable, it will also provide detailed information regarding the performance character-istics of the system. For example, in addition to net profitability, typical feedback from even the most basic testing will illustrate:

- total number of trades;
- number of profitable trades;
- percentage of profitable trades;
- size of largest winning trade;
- size of average winning trade;
- number of losing trades;
- size of largest losing trade;
- size of average losing trade;
- ratio of average win/average loss;
- maximum number of consecutive winning trades;
- length of longest winning period (days, weeks, months, etc);
- length of shortest winning period (days, weeks, months, etc);
- maximum number of consecutive losing trades;
- length of longest losing period (days, weeks, months, etc);
- length of shortest losing period (days, weeks, months, etc);

and so on.

As well as information regarding the overall performance, you can also view and print charts illustrating a simulated profit and loss account, daily percentage swings in your cash and a complete list of all trades, including dates and market entry and exit levels.

Personally, I use the Metastock software computer program produced by Equis International (www.equis.com) and sold through

Paritech (www.paritech.co.uk) to conduct all my research and development. I'm not a geek and even I can operate it. In fact, once you're familiar with how it works, developing and testing systems or ideas takes just a matter of minutes. That said, I'm not recommending that any reader needs to go out and purchase such software, because this book is already providing you with a method to follow, but if you have an interest in exploring system development further, it's not that hard or expensive to do. Also, such testing is very important because, although 'past performance is no indication of future returns', as my hedge fund management company used to have to state in our marketing literature, it is the best indication we have. And through historical testing I've identified that the Long-Term Investment System detailed in this book requires sustained upward trends in the stock market to be profitable. However, thanks to that research, I also know that those trends do not have to be exact replicas of, or even remotely similar to, past price movements for the System to catch and profit from them.

To illustrate this, later in the book I provide the historical performance record of the System covering the last 56 years back to 1951. As you will see, it has proven itself profitable despite the rise and fall of the USSR, the Cold War, conflicts in Korea, Vietnam and the Middle East, the Cuban missile crisis, the assassination of President Kennedy, the resignation of President Nixon, oil crises, currency crises, the sudden market crash of 1987, and numerous acts of terrorism, including the Munich Olympics and 9/11, in addition to some horrible bear markets. It has survived all such crises, booms, bubbles and busts. The System has a long and successful track record, which makes trusting it with your money seem a far more sensible tactic than placing it with a financial 'expert' whose adult memory doesn't stretch back any further than the early 1990s.

# 8

# Disciplined market timing

I find that buying on strength gives you an edge. You may pay a premium, but you increase the probability of being right. According to my rulebook, the only consistent way to make money in the market is to cut losses and run with profits.

(Marty Zweig)

In my experience, all successful stock market strategies have to exploit long-term trends. By long term, I mean sustained upward price movements that last anything up to a few years in duration and, from a profit perspective, the longer the better. Long-term trends such as this are the result of strong fundamentals such as demand outstripping supply; a favourable environment for borrowing money (low interest rates); strong consumer sentiment; and good corporate profits. However, identifying which particular fundamental is the most important at any one time is nigh on impossible, even if you know what to look for.

Thankfully there is no need to concern yourself with such analysis because you can use a market-timing system to direct all your investment decisions. With only a few exceptions, all market-timing strategies involve a practice known as trend following. If you've read my first book or are aware of my work, then you'll know all about trend following and the fact that I'm a strong advocate of using such price momentum-based strategies. The benefit of using any method that's designed to follow price momentum in this way is that it removes many of the difficult decision-making processes, such as when to enter and exit the markets, when to cut your losses, and how to maximize your profits.

> Trend-following systems are simple and adaptable to changing market conditions, thus they have a good chance of working in the future (not just the past).
>
> (Fund Advice.com)

In essence, 'trend-following' strategies or systems do what they say on the label: they seek to identify 'trends' and then 'follow' that movement in prices until there is evidence that the trend is over. Participating in such major price movements should be the goal of every long-term investor because it's the only way for a conservative individual to attain serious profits without taking excessive risk. As the saying goes, 'The big money comes from the big moves.' The real challenge for all of us is to identify such a big move early enough to profit from it, then to participate in that trend for as long as possible and then, finally, to know when to 'leave the party' when the trend has run its course before we give back too much profit.

Thankfully, a strategy based on trend following can help, and it's no coincidence that some of the world's greatest traders, investors and money managers use trend-following strategies. There is plenty of logic to validate the old maxim 'The trend is your friend', and Michael Covel's popular book, the aptly titled *Trend-Following* (see 'Further reading'), is an excellent source of reference for anyone who isn't already familiar with the subject and wants to learn more. Suffice it for me to say that I owe my entire fortune to operating trend-following strategies, and I see no reason for that not to continue.

# 9

# Market timing vs buy and hold

Beware of buy and forget.

(The Motley Fool)

Despite the well-documented success of market-timing/trend-following strategies, there is a school of thought that still believes it's actually impossible to successfully 'time' entries and exits and that a better approach is to simply invest your cash on day one and leave it in the market until such time as either you require the cash back or it has reached a monetary target you have set. This strategy is commonly known as 'buy and hold', and at some point in your own investing career I guarantee you will come across someone who will try to convince you to abandon a systematic market-timing approach in favour of blindly investing your cash and leaving it there until you need the money. Although I have already covered this subject to some degree in my first book, I make no apology for revisiting it and challenging the arguments put forward by the supporters of 'buy and hold'.

Buy-and-hold investors base their strategy upon the premise that over the long run you cannot predict the market's good performing days from the bad, and if you attempt to, then you will end up missing some of the best moves. For example, over the last 20 years, if you had missed the 30 best performing days in the stock market, your portfolio would have underperformed by an average of over 6 per cent per annum. Therefore, their argument is, if you remain invested through all the bull and bear market trends, you ensure that you will always participate in the big price movements whenever they occur.

This all sounds very logical except the theory of buy and hold doesn't take into account the tremendous volatility that stocks can often undergo, the emotional stress and turmoil adverse price movements can cause an investor, and the fact that not all stock indices or individual stocks and shares eventually end higher in price; some collapse and disappear without trace or languish way below their previous valuations. You wouldn't be a very satisfied buy-and-hold investor if your money had been invested in British & Commonwealth Shipping, WorldCom, Brent Walker, Ferranti or Marconi, to name but a few high-profile company collapses. Nor would you be patting yourself on the back if you had been invested in the Japanese stock market during its well-publicized collapse.

A buy-and-hold strategy is extremely dangerous because it doesn't include any rules for liquidating an investment position and therefore fails to offer any protection from a company failure or bear market. Those who follow such an approach have to be prepared to sit through some horrific and emotionally destabilizing price retracements, which in some cases can lead to the complete loss of all monies invested. If your solution to such adverse price movements is to 'think' that you would liquidate an investment if the market turned against you, then you would no longer be a buy-and-hold investor, because the very act of exiting a position owing to a downward movement in price is actually 'market timing'. A true buy-and-hold investor has no strategy for reacting to a movement in prices.

If the argument is still not clear to you, here's another way to think of buy and hold versus market timing. Imagine you had to fly in a make of aircraft that had a reputation for having the odd crash, maybe only once in every 10 years or so, but still the history for this make of plane wasn't flawless. Now if you were offered a parachute, would you accept or decline the offer? Of course, you'd be mad not to take the parachute and have some form of escape if things went wrong. When it comes to investing, following a buy-and-hold strategy is like refusing to accept the offer of a parachute. For example, the 1973–74 bear market saw stocks fall 50 per cent from their highs (see Figure 9.1).

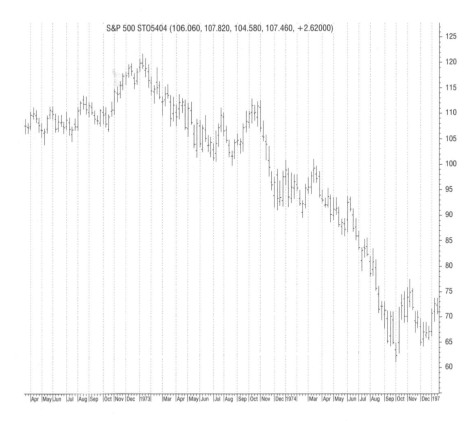

S&P 500 STO5404 (106.060, 107.820, 104.580, 107.460, +2.62000)

**Figure 9.1**    The bear market of 1973-74

At the time, seeing their investment capital halved in a little over 18 months left many investors vowing never to play the markets again. Imagine how you would have felt if you had seen a £10,000 investment become worth just £5,000 and all the press and market experts predicting further falls. Another painful example I often refer to in discussions about this subject is the performance of the NASDAQ Composite Index (a barometer for technology stocks and shares), which rallied from 1,200 in October 1998 to nearly 5,000 by March 2000, during the much-hyped dotcom boom, before collapsing back to 1,200 by September 2001. If you had followed a buy-and-hold approach during this period (see Figure 9.2) you would have remained invested in the market all the way up and then all the way back down again. More than quadrupling your money only to give it all back in the space of a few months is hardly a recipe for long-term success, financial stability or good health!

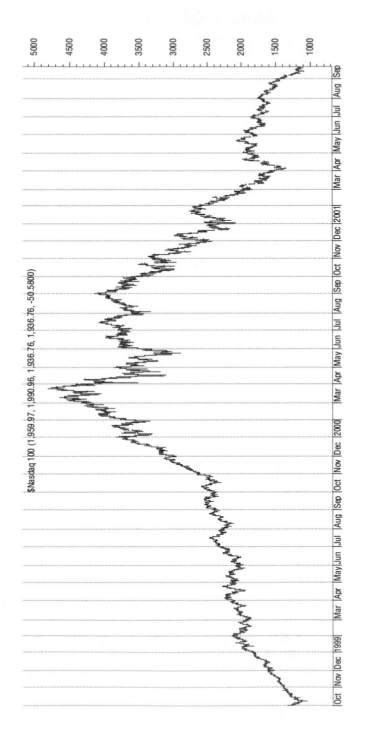

**Figure 9.2** NASDAQ Index October 1998 to September 2001: all the way up and then all the way down

A buy-and-hold approach to investing may feel like a way to seek long-term growth, but it's not a legitimate way to preserve capital because such a strategy has no predetermined rules for liquidating an investment to bank profits or to offer protection if markets enter a sustained bear trend or go into free fall. If you are a buy-and-hold investor you have decided not to take a parachute with you; therefore you must pay the price for your overconfidence and misplaced faith.

Buy and hold = The best of times and the *worst* of times

In contrast, a systematic trend-following approach that 'times' its entries and exits by generating signals based upon price momentum can help to protect investors from the very worst bear markets while still providing them with the opportunity to participate in the big bull market trends whenever they occur. And not only can such a market-timing strategy actually reward an investor with greater overall returns, it can provide those extra profits with less emotional stress and turmoil. In essence, a market-timing strategy is a tool for managing risk. If markets never went down, or if investors never got nervous about paper losses, timing might not be necessary. History confirms, though, that bear markets do occur, and such is their severity that an investor needs some protection. Such a 'parachute' not only helps to protect our capital and emotions from the ravages of a sustained fall in stock market values; it also ensures we 'keep our powder dry', ready for whenever the next big investment opportunity occurs. The end result is far superior performance returns with less stress.

To illustrate this, let's compare how buy-and-hold investors would have fared against those operating the Long-Term Investment System over the last major stock market bull and bear trends. Beginning in January 1995, investors who have decided to adopt a buy-and-hold approach invest in the S&P 500 Composite Index, which consists of the top 500 companies in the United States. The level of the index at the time was around 460, and this is where they invested £10,000 in the market. By March 2000, the market had rallied to 1,525, representing a gain of 230 per cent on their original investment, but as they are buy-and-hold investors they continue to 'hold' their position. Unfortunately, the market then proceeds to collapse to 800 by the middle of 2002. From this low the S&P then rallies back to 1,530 by the summer of 2007, which is just above the peak level the market had originally hit seven years earlier. So, as buy-and-hold investors they would have experienced unrealized gains of 230 per cent, lost almost half of that during a vicious bear market and then finally recovered those losses as the market returned to new highs. The total value of their investment capital now stands at £33,260, which represents a 230 per cent plus gain over this 12-year roller-coaster ride. Although the return looks impressive on paper, the buy-and-holders would have undoubtedly suffered high emotional cost through the stress and sleepless nights they would have experienced when the market collapsed between 2000 and 2003. And anybody who tells you they would have slept like a baby as their investment cash lost nearly half of its value is being less than truthful. Figure 9.3 illustrates the bull–bear–bull trends the market underwent during this 12-year period.

In contrast, let's review the performance of investors using a market-timing strategy such as the Long-Term Investment System and establishing an identical £10,000 investment at the same time and price as the buy-and-holders. The System would have remained invested in the market until a sell signal was generated at the beginning of 2001 at around the 1,280 level. Reacting to this signal, the market-timing investors would have liquidated their investment and then banked their original investment cash plus a 178 per cent profit from the trade into a savings account to earn interest for the next few years whilst the stock market collapsed. Then, when a buy signal was finally generated in the middle of 2003 around the 990 level, they would have established a new position, investing their original starting capital (£10,000) plus the banked profits from the first trade (£17,800) plus the bank interest earned from the previous three years when their cash had safely remained in an interest-bearing account (at a conservative interest rate of 4 per cent per annum this would equate to approximately £3,000). Therefore, adding these amounts together, the total of their new investment would be around £30,800, which would have been reinvested into the S&P in the summer of 2003 at around the 990 price level. The market then rallied for the next 18 months until the System

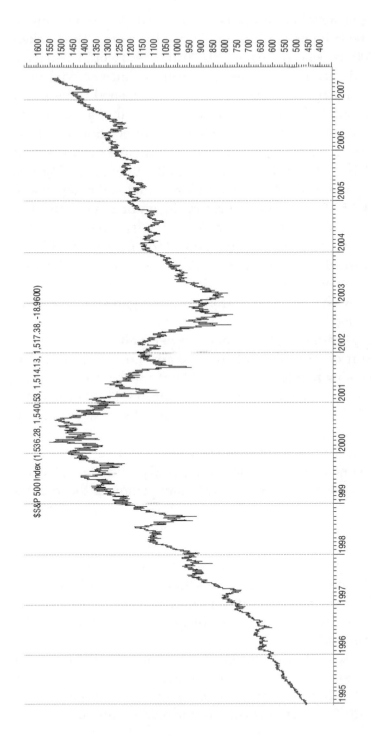

**Figure 9.3** S&P 500 Index 1995–2007

generated a sell signal in November 2004 at 1,130. The investment would have been liquidated for a gain of 14 per cent. The banked profit of £4,300 (14 per cent on the £30,800 invested) would then have been deposited back into an interest-bearing savings account until the next buy signal was generated, which happened to be just a month later around Christmas 2004. Acting upon this signal, a new investment of £35,100 (capital invested in the last position of £30,800 plus the profit it generated of £4,300) would have been made at around the 1,195 index price level and, at the time of writing this book in the summer of 2007, this position would still be open at a price level of 1,530, posting an unrealized gain of 28 per cent. The unrealized profit on this position stands at £9,900 (28 per cent on the £35,100 invested). In total, using the Long-Term Investment System would have turned a £10,000 investment in 1995 into £45,000, representing a net gain of 350 per cent.

Let's compare the financial performance of both strategies over the 12-year period.

The market-timing approach made a net gain of 350 per cent versus a profit of 230 per cent for buy-and-hold. Additionally, investors following market timing would not only have had a larger amount of money invested in the market of £45,000 (original investment of £10,000 plus banked profits from the closed trades of £17,800 and £4,300 plus savings account interest of £3,000 plus unrealized profits by the summer of 2007 of £9,900) versus £33,260 (original investment of £10,000 plus unrealized profits of £23,260) for the buy-and-holders, but they would have enjoyed those extra profits without having had to sit through one of the worst bear markets in recent history, missing all the emotional pressures that would have plagued the buy-and-hold investors.

Figure 9.4 compares the equity swings of a buy-and-hold investor with the performance of an investor who followed the Long-Term Investment System and provides an excellent illustration of the different fortunes experienced by the two strategies over exactly the same 12-year period.

For the first six years, the performance returns were identical, but observe the changes in fortune of each strategy as the S&P 500 began its bear market in 2000. As you can see, from this point until the next buy signal in 2003, the performance of the market-timing approach

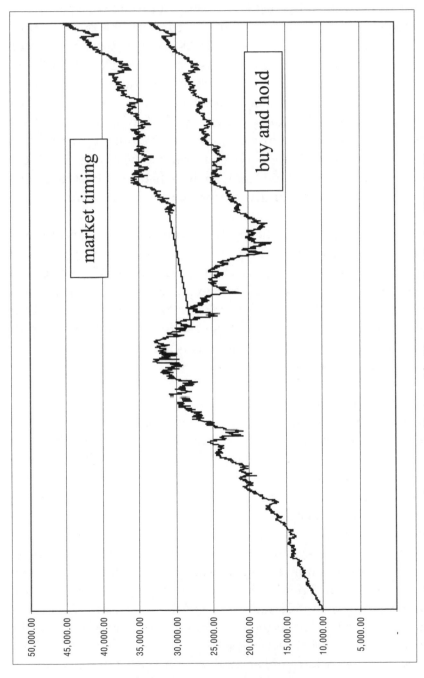

**Figure 9.4** Comparative performance of buy and hold versus market timing 1995–2007

enjoyed a steady period of growth from £28,000 to £30,800 owing to the interest it received whilst its investment capital was 'parked' in an interest-bearing savings account. In contrast, the buy-and-hold strategy saw its equity drop from £33,000 to £17,000, as it remained invested throughout the three-year-long bear market. This divergence in the performance of the two strategies graphically illustrates the serious advantage market timing has over buy and hold when markets perform badly. And even though the buy-and-hold method recovered its bear market losses as the S&P 500 rallied from its 2003 low to its 2007 highs, it is always now going to be playing catch-up. This is because the market-timing strategy had protected its capital during the bear trend and therefore had considerably more to reinvest in the recovery.

One-and-a-half times the profit for far less stress, and that's assuming the buy-and-holders would have remained invested throughout the collapse in prices between 2000 and 2003, which is a big ask of anyone. In fact, this example flatters the performance of buy and holding, because the S&P ultimately reversed its bear market and rallied to new highs. If that hadn't happened, a buy-and-hold strategy would have underperformed market timing by an even greater margin. Just imagine how you would have suffered if you'd applied buy and hold to the NASDAQ during the boom-and-bust cycle we examined earlier in this chapter.

The major flaw in the argument for a buy-and-hold strategy is its failure to accept and provide for the many occasions when markets fall in value. Following such an approach means you will be 'running your profits and *running your losses*', which goes starkly against the common investment wisdom of 'running your profits and cutting your losses'. If you decide to use buy and hold, you need to be fully aware of the tremendous financial risks and psychological pressures the strategy entails, because whenever the market enters a bear trend, which it does every now and again, such an approach will offer you no protection whatsoever from catastrophic losses. In contrast, market timing invariably reduces the risk of investing, because it requires investors to have their money in cash at least some of the time during the market's worst-performing periods. Every day your money is not at risk in a bear market, you place the odds in your favour that you will avoid the very worst market movements and, in a bull market, every day that your money is invested the odds favour that you will enjoy some of the strongest market price movements. This is important because, to paraphrase the respected market commentator, trader and investor David Fuller, 'In a bull market, most of the surprises will be on the upside, and in a bear market most of the surprises will be on the downside.'

In summary, the chief advantage of market timing is that you don't leave your wealth completely exposed to the risk of the market all the time. In addition, following a system such as the one detailed in this book not only removes some of the stress from stock market investing but also helps to reduce downside volatility, lowers the long-term risk on your investments, helps you to remain emotionally stable and, most important of all, increases your chances of making money. And if you ever encounter another long-term bear market, you know that you have a 'parachute' to protect you, which gives you a serious financial and psychological advantage.

# 10

# The psychology of following a system

Systems work; it's people that don't!

(Steve Sheen)

Although systematic investing may sound very clinical, we mustn't lose sight of the fact that systems still have to be operated by human beings, with all their quirks, emotions and indiscipline. Whether you're using a systematic approach or not, investing *without* discipline is a highly stressful experience and ultimately leads to poor decisions, especially at moments of intense pressure, when we tend to rely more upon our emotions than our intellect. Although we are all flesh and blood, emotions should play no part in your decision-making process, and once you have committed to following a systematic strategy you must ensure you execute every signal it generates. Failure to follow the rules means you are interfering with a tried-and-tested approach, which is not only illogical but also extremely dangerous to your wealth.

The System in this book is successful; it has proven itself profitable both historically and in real time. It has a positive expectancy; but, for you to make it work, you have to follow its rules *without fail*. Some of you will be able to do this better than others, and the main difference between the systematic investors who succeed and those who do not will be down to personal discipline. The psychological side of speculation is a subject that deserves a book in its own right, and although we've already covered some of the problems that can beset an investor, I'd like to quickly review the pressures that could trip you up from a systematic perspective.

The first psychologically based trap that many systematic investors fall into is the failure to follow a signal when their system has generated one. Failing to act upon a system signal is a cardinal sin. It is no good having your system generate a signal only for you to wait a while to 'see if it works out'. By then the market could have accelerated higher, and a major investment opportunity would have been lost. And if you fall foul of such procrastination, it's almost psychologically impossible to then establish that position later on at a higher market price because that would be an admission to yourself that you should have acted earlier and failed.

Another psychological trap many fall into is when an investor anticipates a system signal. During your investment career there will be occasions when the market moves close to a level where you know that your system is close to generating either a buy or a sell signal. When such a scenario occurs do not allow yourself to 'second-guess' the system by opening or closing a position before the signal has been generated. It might feel clever to invest earlier and obtain a better price level in the market rather than wait for the buy signal or to exit the market at a slightly higher level before the system generates a sell signal, but you are breaking the rules and this is a dangerous modus operandi. On the few occasions where you might make a small additional profit or save yourself a bit of extra cash by second-guessing a system, you also run the risk of being caught out if the market never actually hits your system's trigger level. Acting in advance of a system signal and then witnessing the market failing to reach the actual target price level may cost you far more, both psychologically and financially. For example, if you act in advance of a buy signal you could find yourself invested in a market that then fails to move higher or, even worse, heads in the opposite direction. You now hold an investment position that's losing money because you're involved in a market that you shouldn't have participated in. Likewise, if you act in advance of a sell signal, you could liquidate a sound investment position on a minor retracement and then find yourself watching the market resume its bull market trend; only now you no longer have a position.

A third trap is to listen to someone else, especially an 'armchair investor', and let that person's opinion override the signal your system has generated. Just as 'armchair sports spectators' are 'experts' regarding the sport they're watching on the television, similarly you may run into the occasional 'armchair investor' who holds strong opinions on how you are investing your money. For instance, imagine you are down the pub, in the gym or at a dinner party, when you announce to your friends that you are going to control your own investments in the stock market using a systematic strategy. Typically, following a sharp intake of breath, your friends will try to interfere and offer their own 'advice' on investing or, even worse, give you a 'hot tip' they've received from a stockbroker mate. This is when the warning bells should ring because unless the people concerned have made their fortune from investing, you should ignore them! They may have strong views or speak very loudly, but what do they know? It's amazing how confusing things can get if you listen to other people instead of simply following your own approach. Whenever you bump into such 'know-it-alls', always remember that there are not many people you can trust when it comes to advice on investing, because there are very few people who have the knowledge and have actually made a success of it. Unless the people offering you their wisdom can prove they are among the successful elite, put your hands over your ears or get as far away from them as quickly as possible.

If you decide to operate and follow the signals of a system, then do just that. Don't ignore the signals because you think you know better this time; don't second-guess or anticipate any signals for the same reason; and don't listen to the opinions of well-meaning but ultimately ignorant 'armchair investors'. The Long-Term Investment System has performed very well for the last five decades without your help or interference, and it doesn't need any of that input now. Successful investing is the result of patience and discipline: the patience to wait for your strategy to indicate when to participate; the discipline to then act upon that signal; the patience to hold on to that investment position, maximizing any profit; and, finally, the discipline to act upon the signal that tells you to liquidate, whether for a profit or a loss. Keep your emotions in check and out of the market. Remember, good systems do not fail, only the people who operate them.

# 11

# Is that all there is?

Early in my career I made an observation about human nature and money – that people tend to complicate something in direct proportion to its importance. [This] helps to explain why over two-thirds of professional investors fail to beat the market averages even though they spend heavily on research, employ economists, follow hundreds of companies, have sophisticated computer models and use techniques like program trading to try to enhance returns and limit losses.

(Michael O'Higgins)

It's a fact of market speculation that the majority of participants complicate what is essentially a very simple subject. It doesn't matter whether they're using fundamental analysis, technical analysis or a combination of the two; most people generally dig too deep when they try to solve the conundrum of the markets. It is no coincidence that most of the world's top investors and traders operate KISS (Keep It Simple, Stupid) strategies.

In a sense, it's easy to see why the majority try to over-complicate things. From our very earliest memories, we are taught that 'hard work equals success', and this mantra is then repeated throughout our formal education and into full-time employment. However, successful investing is different. It's about 'working smart, not working hard'. This is a concept that many find hard to accept, and I still have trouble convincing people that I can make as much money as, if not more money than, the majority of professionals by 'working' less than one hour a week. I can see how it does seem unbelievable, especially if you compare my 60 minutes' worth of effort a week to that of a City professional who has to wake up at 5.45 am to get the train to work and then sits in front of a quote screen or reads reports all day until it's time to go home, which is typically just in time to put the kids to bed. I know that my claims embarrassingly sound like one of those mailshots we all get from time to time with headlines or banners such as 'Retire rich for just one hour's work a week', but in my case this is the truth. Hard work may be the secret to success in other professions, but when it comes to successful investing discipline, patience and a simple set of proven rules are all anyone needs.

The markets can only go up, down or sideways, and as an investor you have only one decision to make: to participate or not. If you accept that successful investing is more about running profits, cutting losses and maintaining the discipline to do just that, then you'll understand why your strategy for investing doesn't need to be too complicated and incorporate too many 'bells and whistles', as we say in the trade. Essentially, any good system that follows long-term trends and forces you to invest in assets that are rising in value and keep away from those that are falling will be good enough to outperform most investors. Historically, the System in this book has done just that. When you read the rules, do not be put off by their apparent simplicity, because systems such as this have been successfully used by professionals for decades, and my own personal experience confirms that simple is best. I've even tried to prove otherwise!

Back in the 1990s, when my hedge fund management company began to grow in size, we conducted numerous in-house research and development projects. Using the expertise of highly educated, computer-literate 'boffins' with state-of-the-art computers and software, my company researched hundreds of different and diverse trading and investing strategies. We tested every type of market-related idea on decades of minute, daily, weekly and monthly data, including: chart pattern recognition algorithms; guru-based analysis such as Gann and Elliott Wave; popular technical indicators such as MACD, RSI and parabolic analysis; Fibonacci levels; and even statistical analysis of fundamental information such as P/E ratios, dividend yields and government data.

The results were interesting, to say the least. No matter how 'clever' we became dreaming up different algorithms and filters, we found that, beyond using around two to four key rules, performance always began to suffer. With just one or two exceptions, increasing the filters we placed upon a signal to protect us from losses actually resulted in us missing some very profitable opportunities as well. In fact, almost every new attempt we made to protect a portfolio from loss actually led to a reduction in overall net profitability. In short, we found it nigh on impossible to fine-tune our already successful strategies any further. Our research proved that the most important criterion was to have an unambiguous method for identifying serious shifts in price momentum, either up or down, and the more we tried to perfect such strategies, the more we over-complicated matters, which generally resulted in reduced profitability.

In summary, this research and development project identified that if you want to operate a method that will guarantee you never miss a major market trend, then you need to keep it simple. To use a phrase I often include in my presentations, 'The market doesn't go up just because it has satisfied one of my rules, but a line needs to be drawn in the sand somewhere, and if you can historically prove that the rules you are using have worked in the past, then that's where the line is drawn.' It's important that you operate an approach that almost guarantees your participation in every major bull market, because missing such a trend could mean the difference between long-term success and failure. And don't be put off the Long-Term Investment System by comments like 'Oh, it's just a simple moving average crossover; they've been around for years', because when it comes to speculating in the markets you need just such a KISS (Keep It Simple, Stupid) approach. To quote Dennis Tilley, Head of Investment Research at FundAdvice.com, 'There are advantages to simplicity. Many timing models incorporate more information and more complicated trading rules, but they carry a higher risk of over-optimizing to the past. Even with superb back-tested results, when complex, sophisticated timing systems are used in real time they often underperform simpler ones.'

Your focus is to make money. Let the 'clever' people continue with their esoteric, complicated and ultimately underperforming strategies. However, if you're still undecided about the validity of such a straightforward strategy as the Long-Term Investment System, let me introduce you to 'the Turtles'.

# 12

# The Turtles

Within the small community of successful fund managers lies a group of individuals collectively known as 'the Turtles'. Their story is legendary and should act as an inspiration to all who are interested in using simple and practical systems to speculate in the markets. And anyone familiar with the 1985 hit film *Trading Places*, starring Eddie Murphy, Dan Ackroyd and Jamie Lee Curtis, may be interested to learn just how close the film's theme is to the original true story of the Turtles. It all began around the summer of 1983, in Chicago, Illinois, when two learned gentlemen decided to settle their long-running debate about whether the skills required to be a successful trader and investor were teachable or a gift. It was an age-old question that's been applied to many supposedly skill-based occupations: nature or nurture?

In the blue corner was Richard Dennis, probably at the time the world's most famous futures trader, with a personal fortune in the tens of millions, and in the red corner his lifelong friend and a very successful trader in his own right, Bill Eckhardt. Dennis believed that great traders weren't born; they could be made by reducing the 'skills' of a successful trader to a set of simple, easy-to-follow rules. Eckhardt thought that genetics was the determining factor and that good market speculation was more the result of some mystical, subjective or intuitive input.

In order to settle their disagreement once and for all, they decided to conduct an intellectual experiment. It was to become the most famous experiment in the history of market speculation, and the ramifications are still felt today, not least with the publication of this book. Dennis suggested that they recruit a group of people from all walks of life and teach them how to trade the markets; then he would allow each one to manage some of his money. The performance of the group would determine if good traders and investors are born or if they can be created. Eckhardt agreed, and they placed a large advertisement for trading apprentices in the *Wall Street Journal*, the *New York Times* and *Barron's*. The advert stated that the only prerequisites were that the applicant should have a basic understanding of mathematics and a love of playing games. The advertisement attracted over a thousand responses, which Dennis whittled down to less than a hundred individuals, whom he personally interviewed. Finally Dennis reduced the list to 13 people, including an accountant, two professional gamblers, a fantasy game designer, an engineer, an actor, a security guard and a juggler!

At the end of December 1983, the experiment began in earnest when the successful applicants were invited to Chicago to sign a 10-year secrecy agreement and then spend the next two weeks being trained by Dennis. In essence, he taught the students a simple trend-following system, and by the beginning of January 1984 they were allowed to trade very small amounts of Dennis's personal fortune using the system. By February, each successful trainee received further funding from Dennis of between $500,000 and $2 million. Dennis christened this group of newly trained novices 'the Turtles'. He had just returned from Asia prior to starting the experiment and described his trading academy to a journalist by saying 'We are going to grow traders just like they grow turtles in Singapore', and so the Turtles had begun their journey into trading folklore.

To cut a long story short, the results of the experiment were outstanding and indeed proved that good traders and investors can be created. As Dennis remarked at the time, 'Trading was even more teachable than I imagined. In a strange sort of way, it was almost humbling.' In fact, the experiment was so successful that, to prove it was no fluke, Dennis repeated it the following year with a second group of 10 students. Over the next few years, the Turtles amassed excellent profits, which led many of them to amicably leave Dennis and branch out, establishing their own fund management businesses, and to this day some of the most successful traders, investors and hedge fund managers in the world are former Turtles. Names such as Jerry Parker, Paul Rabar and Liz Cheval are legendary amongst the alternative fund management industry, with billions of dollars under their control. To quote from one of the original Turtles, Curtis Faith (in the manual 'The original Turtles system'), 'Rich proved that trading could be taught. He proved that, with a simple set of rules, he could take people with little or no trading experience and make them excellent traders.'

The Turtles' story should be an inspiration to any reader who is considering trading or investing for the first time. It can be done. Richard Dennis proved it with a diverse and unusual collection of individuals and a simple trend-following system not that dissimilar in principle to the Long-Term Investment System. The Turtles were taught a strategy that forced them to follow price momentum, and for them the rest is history. Now it's your turn. None of this is rocket science; you don't need a degree in anything, and if you can operate a computer, access the internet and understand the basic operation of a calculator you're well equipped to succeed. Take it from someone who has.

Now for the System.

# 13

# The Long-Term Investment System

At the end of World War II, by which time much of my present investment philosophy was largely formulated, I had made what I believe was one of the more valuable decisions of my business life. This was to confine all efforts solely to making major gains over the long run.

(Philip A Fisher, 1996)

It's been my experience that the real big money is made from participating in major long-term trends, and that's why the majority of the strategies I have developed and use focus upon identifying and participating in such market movements. The method we are about to review is no different and, as with most of the technical strategies I operate, I credit Richard Donchian, one of the pioneers of investment system design, as the inspiration for its development. He was one of the first people to recognize the value of developing trend-following systems to trade the markets, and I have found that my most effective strategies normally incorporate at least one of his philosophies. Donchian was very fond of using moving averages, and it's no coincidence that even nowadays they form the cornerstone of many a successful technical strategy, including the Long-Term Investment System.

# Moving averages

Moving averages (MA) are one of the most basic yet effective trend-following technical analysis tools available to the investor. Essentially, all a moving average does is smooth out the price fluctuations of a market by averaging the closing prices for a certain period of time to provide a clearer visual picture of the major market trends over the same period. For example, a 50-week MA would indicate the average weekly closing price of the last 50 weeks and, if it's increasing in value, this normally indicates that the market is gaining long-term upward (bullish) momentum. Conversely, if the 50-week MA begins to fall in value, this normally indicates long-term downward (bearish) momentum. Because manually recording the necessary amount of weekly data to construct such long-term moving averages is going to take you nearly a year, I would encourage you to use the internet to program them. There are a number of free access websites that enable you to monitor moving averages without any long-winded record keeping, and later on I will take you step by step through the website procedures. Although I would not encourage you to adopt the manual process of calculating moving averages, I'll quickly review the process so you understand exactly how they are constructed.

To manually calculate a 50-week MA, you need the weekly closing price (this is the closing price of the market on the last trading day of the week, typically a Friday except for the odd bank holiday) for the most recent 50 weeks. Then to calculate a moving average figure, you simply add up those 50 weekly closing prices and divide the cumulative figure by 50 (the number of weeks in the data sample). This final figure represents the current 50-week MA (the average weekly closing price for the last 50 weeks). In the following weeks, to update the current 50-week MA figure, simply repeat the process by adding up the most recent 50 weeks' closing prices and then divide by 50. This calculation is repeated at the end of every trading week. That's how to manually calculate a moving average, but unless you're really into record keeping and number crunching I recommend you use the internet and have all this laborious work done for you.

Way before I was born, Richard Donchian was successfully managing customer funds with a system that utilized two moving averages. Applied to the commodity and futures markets, the basis of the system was that whenever a 5-day MA had a higher figure than a 20-day MA the market should be bought, and whenever a 5-day MA had a lower figure than a 20-day MA the market should be sold. His system ensured that, if a major trend occurred in either direction, Donchian and his clients would participate and reap the rewards. Over the years since he first developed and operated such systems, many traders and investors have adapted Donchian's work and added other confirming filters or altered the timeframe of the moving averages. Shorter-term traders usually utilize hourly or daily moving averages, which will indicate the market's most recent dynamics, whereas longer-term investors normally focus on weekly timeframes.

Although Donchian's moving average systems were and still are successful, they occasionally fall foul of the curse of any approach based on trend following, namely the non-trending market. It's widely accepted that markets can spend a large percentage of their time without any sustained trends, and these non-trending periods often create numerous false buy and sell signals known in market terminology as 'whipsaws'. It can be both frustrating and financially painful when your strategy hits just such a period of price action, so, to avoid some of these whipsaw signals, many system developers either require the market to meet additional criteria before a buy or sell signal is taken or extend the time frames the moving averages cover, making them less sensitive to shorter-term price fluctuations. The Long-Term Investment System focuses upon the latter option, as I have found that using a combination of longer-term moving averages, such as 30 weeks and 50 weeks, helps to considerably reduce whipsaws while still allowing participation in the strongest trends. So here are the rules. Don't blink; otherwise you might miss them!

# 14

# The rules

In the most simplistic of ways, you can think of this as a method that instructs you either to invest your money in the stock market or to place it in an instant access interest-bearing savings account (cash). It seeks to keep your money in the stock market when prices are moving higher and in cash when they're not.

A **'buy (invest in the stock market)'** signal is active whenever the most recent **30-week** moving average figure is **greater (higher)** than the most recent **50-week** moving average figure.

A **'sell (savings account investment)'** signal is active whenever the most recent **50-week** moving average figure is **greater (higher)** than the most recent **30-week** moving average figure.

To summarize these rules, when the average weekly closing price for the last *30* weeks is a *higher* figure than the average weekly closing price for the last *50* weeks, there is a strong probability that the stock market will move higher in the long term and it is in your interest to invest. In essence, the System forces you to draw a line in the sand that, once crossed, indicates a potentially bullish environment has been entered. Conversely, when the average weekly closing price for the last *50* weeks is a *higher* figure than the average weekly closing price for the last *30* weeks, there is a strong probability that the stock market will move lower in the long term and it's in your interest to close any outstanding positions to prevent you incurring losses from a downward movement in prices. Through both historical research and actual experience, I have found this strategy to be an effective way of participating in some great bull markets, while avoiding some of the worst bear markets.

For the avoidance of doubt, and I apologize to any readers if I'm teaching them to suck eggs, the System can only be in one of two signal conditions: a 'buy' signal is active or a 'sell' signal is active. Always use the 'buy' signal to invest in the stock market and the 'sell' signal to reduce your stock market exposure to zero and invest your cash in an interest-bearing savings account with a well-known and respectable institution. This might seem obvious but if you already hold a stock market position and your weekly analysis generates a 'buy' signal, no further action is required, because you are already participating in the market; and, conversely, if you do not hold a position when your weekly analysis indicates a 'sell' signal, no further action is required, because you have no position to get out of!

# 15

# An operational guide

The most efficient way to operate the System requires access to a computer and an internet connection.

You will track the price movements of the stock market index of your choice on a weekly basis, using one of the most basic tools of technical analysis, a chart. A chart is basically a visual representation of a market's price movements over a specified time frame. Those readers who are not completely conversant with using charts may wish to review a couple of well-known books, Edwards and Magee's *Technical Analysis of Stock Trends* and John Murphy's *Technical Analysis of the Futures Markets* (see 'Further reading'). I personally use and recommend internet charts because they reduce the amount of record keeping, as you are not required to record every weekly close nor are you required to manually calculate the moving averages. Another benefit of using the internet is that you can begin operating the System from day one without having to build up the required historical records, which on a manual basis would take approximately one year.

The type of chart you will use is known as a 'bar chart', where a single vertical bar on the chart displays a market's open, high, low and closing price for a specific period.

As illustrated in Figure 15.1, the top of each vertical bar (H) represents the highest price the market has traded during the period; the bottom of the bar (L) represents the lowest price it has traded; and the small horizontal dash displayed on the right-hand side of the bar (C) represents the closing price for that period. On some bar charts, you may also find a small horizontal dash displayed on the left-hand

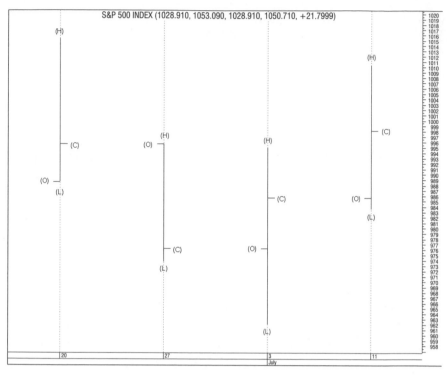

**Figure 15.1** A bar chart

side of the bar, which represents the opening price (O). All bar charts display their historical data in the same way, with the oldest data on the far left of the chart through to the most recent market movement detailed on the far right. Visually, we do not actually require the open, high, low or close information, but it is included in this guide so you are more familiar with the workings of a bar chart when you see one. Our point of focus on a bar chart will be the interaction between the two continuous moving average lines that weave left to right across the chart, as illustrated in Figure 15.2.

Bar charts can be used to represent any period from one minute, where each bar covers just a minute's price information, up to a year, where a single bar can represent a whole year. To operate the System, you will need to focus upon a weekly bar chart, where each bar represents a single week's price movement and the moving averages are calculated using weekly closing prices. There are a number of good websites that allow free access for the programming of weekly bar charts, and a quick scan using an internet search facility will

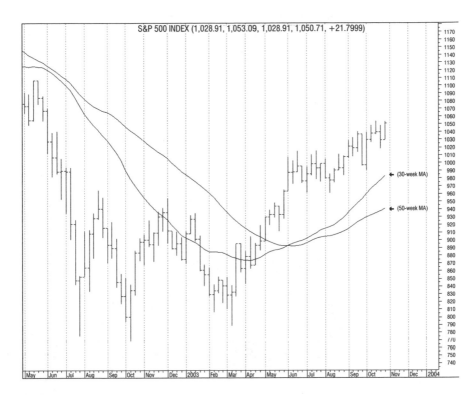

**Figure 15.2**   A bar chart with moving averages

detail those currently available. I personally use the free access website www.futuresource.com to conduct my weekly analysis, and I've written the following step-by-step guide to help those unfamiliar with this website to navigate themselves through the process of tracking the world's main stock indices.

First of all, type in the web address www.futuresource.com, which will direct you to the website home page (see Figure 15.3).

Double-left-click on the word 'Charts', which is located half-way down the page below a small icon of a graph. This will take you to the charts page (see Figure 15.4).

Beneath the chart under the title 'Contract', there are a number of boxes, and this is where the rest of the website programming will be. Click on the down arrow on the box next to 'Choose Contract:' and this will bring up a list of all the markets monitored by this website. Scroll down to select the market you wish to monitor and left-click on the name. As at the time of going to press, this website covered the following stock market indices:

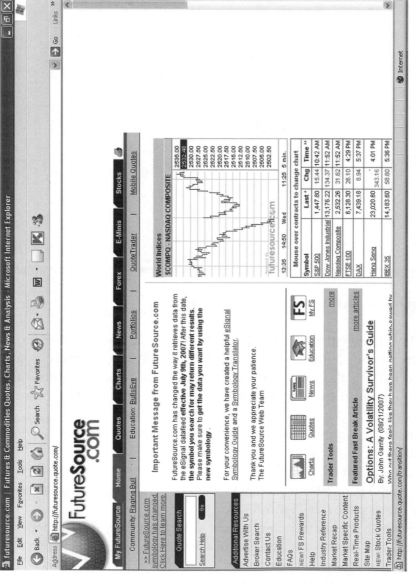

**Figure 15.3** FutureSource.com home page

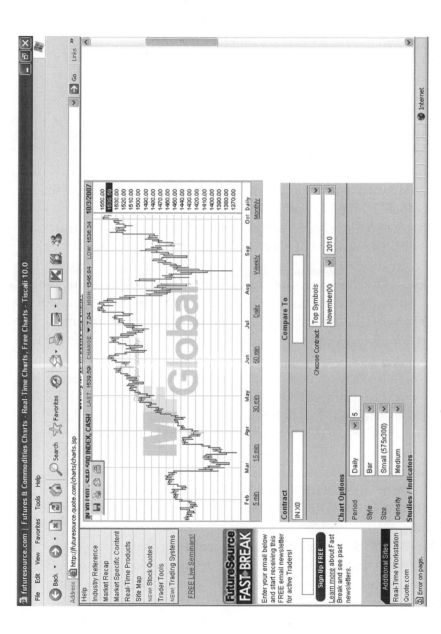

**Figure 15.4** FutureSource.com charts page

| | |
|---|---|
| CAC 40 Stock | France |
| DAX Index | Germany |
| Dow Jones Industrial | United States |
| FTSE 100 | United Kingdom |
| Hang Seng | Hong Kong |
| NASDAQ-100 | United States |
| Nikkei 225 (IOM) | Japan |
| SP 500 | United States |

(Further information about each stock market index, including lists of component companies, can be found later in the book.)

Then go to the box beneath and left-click on the down arrow – this will bring up a list of calendar months. Scroll up to the top of the list and left-click on the word 'Month'.

Then go to the box on the right and left-click on the down arrow – this will bring up a list of years. Scroll up to the top of the list and left-click on the word 'Year'. The page should now look like Figure 15.5.

Next go to the bottom of the web page to the boxes beneath the title 'Studies/Indicators'. In the box under the title 'Available:', double-left-click on 'Moving Average (4, 9, 18)'. This will make the word 'Moving Average' appear in the box on the right under the title 'Selected:'.

Now left-click on that word and beneath it, in the three boxes below next to the title 'Parameters:', the numbers '4', '9' and '18' will appear, as shown in Figure 15.6.

Next click on each of the three boxes and change the numbers as follows. In the first box, left-click to the right of the number and change it from '4' to '30'. In the middle box, do the same and change the number from '9' to '50', and in the third and final box change the number from '18' to '50'. The three boxes should now read from left to right '30', '50' and '50'.

Now go back up the page and, beneath the chart, double-left-click on the word 'Weekly'. This will bring up the weekly chart of the stock market index you wish to monitor, complete with two moving average lines weaving across the chart. One coloured line represents the 30-week MA and the other coloured line represents the 50-week MA, with a colour code identifying which line represents which

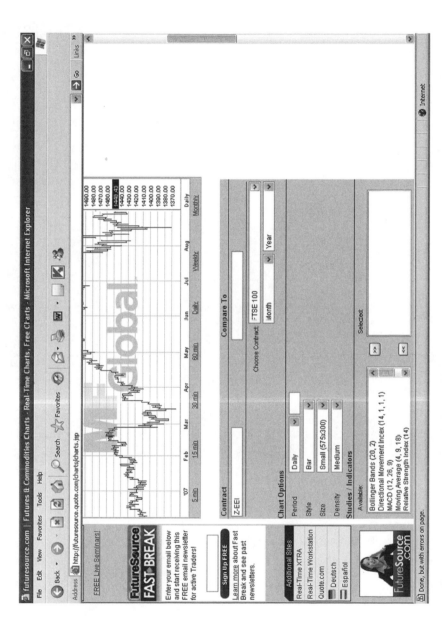

**Figure 15.5** FutureSource.com chart page programmed with stock index information

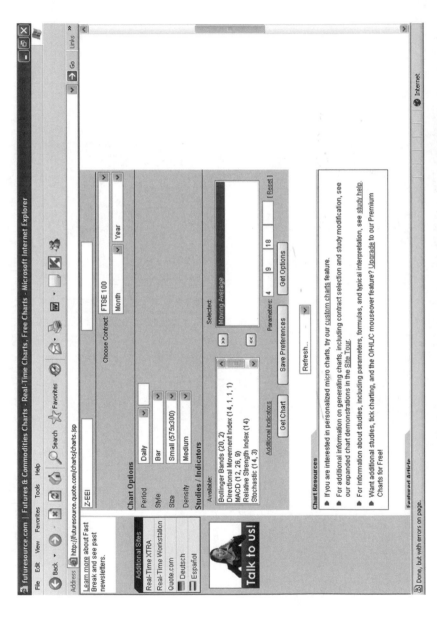

**Figure 15.6** FutureSource.com chart page programmed with moving average study

moving average and their values displayed across the top of the chart, as shown in Figure 15.7.

Now you are ready to conduct the System analysis. When using bar charts to monitor for signals, ignore all the other information detailed on the chart and just focus upon the two moving average lines and their relationship on the extreme right-hand side of the chart, because this represents the most recent moving average values. The example in Figure 15.7 is a 'buy' signal, because the 30-week moving average line (30-week MA) is higher than the 50-week moving average line (50-week MA) on the far right-hand side of the chart. For a 'sell' signal to be active, the 50-week moving average line would have to be higher than the 30-week moving average line on the far right-hand side of the chart.

To repeat your analysis for another market, simply change the stock market index next to the 'Choose Contract:' box and double-left-click on the word 'Weekly' beneath the chart.

This 'free access' website will provide you with all the information you require to operate the System. It covers most of the major stock market indices in the world, and the data is both accurate and easy to use once you've had some practice. And when you're proficient in programming the website, the whole weekly process shouldn't take you more than 10 minutes to complete even if you are monitoring four or five stock market indices. 'Little effort', as it says on the cover.

Another useful piece of advice when using an internet charting service is *not* to conduct your online analysis until the market has closed for the week. This may sound blindingly obvious, but any analysis conducted before the market has closed for the week will not be accurate, as it will not contain the correct weekly closing price, owing to the fact that the market has not actually finished trading yet! Personally, all my weekly analysis is completed on a Saturday or Sunday, which ensures not only that the market has finished trading for the week but also that I am perfectly clear what action is required when the market reopens at the beginning of the next week.

Another alternative for conducting your analysis is to purchase a charting software package and download the data via the internet. If this is the route you wish to take then the Metastock software program mentioned earlier in the book is a good source of product.

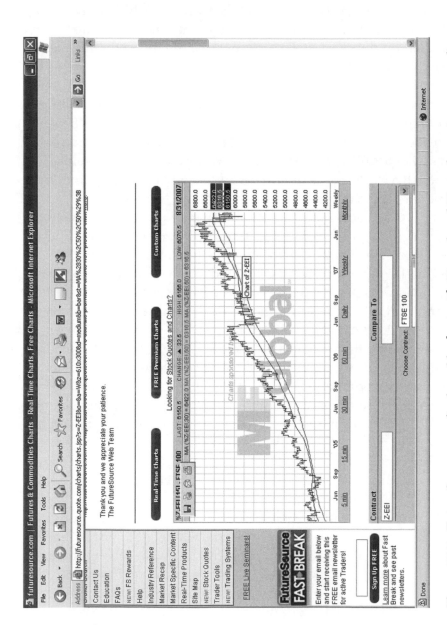

**Figure 15.7** FutureSource.com final weekly chart with 30-week and 50-week moving average lines

# 16

# Where to invest – asset allocation

It's a widely held belief that the real key to long-term success in investing is where you place your money. Such strategic planning goes under the grand-sounding title of 'asset allocation'. Essentially, if you invest your cash in the wrong asset class, you will underachieve and your financial future will be less prosperous. Deciding the correct asset or assets in which to invest money for long-term gains is a problem that besets all investors. This book seeks to provide the reader with a disciplined investment strategy that deals with the most important allocation risks associated with investing: market risk, security risk and product risk.

'Market risk' is the risk of when you invest your cash. The timing of when you participate in a trend is essential, because if you have invested in an asset that is losing value you increase the risk of losing some of your money – not a pleasant or rewarding experience. All major asset classes suffer from bear markets at some point or another, and a large percentage of your long-term success is going to be the result of simply keeping your cash out of an asset that's in a bear market, while remaining invested when there is a bull market. A robust market-timing strategy should be designed to do just that: to clearly and simply indicate whether the long-term trend of the stock market is upwards, which means you should invest, or whether the long-term trend of the stock market is down, in which case you should keep your money out of the market and in a safe interest-bearing savings account.

'Security risk' is the risk of where you invest your cash. Should it be in just one or two individual stocks, a stock market sector or the overall market? This is security risk. For example, over a 12-month period from the beginning of April 2003, the Dow Jones Industrial Average, an index consisting of the 30 largest companies in the United States, rallied over 30 per cent. However, let us suppose you thought that the Dow was going to have a positive year but decided to 'cherry-pick' one particular company in the hope that it would outperform the average. Microsoft (MSFT) looked an interesting candidate, a multibillion-dollar business with operations around the globe, combined with good management. But by just selecting one stock you now have security risk, the risk that you may be correct about the overall direction of the general market but that you may have invested your money in the wrong asset, in this case an under-performing individual stock. Well, between April 2003 and March 2004, that's what happened. The Dow Jones Industrials posted an impressive 30 per cent plus gain over the 12-month period, yet the shares of Microsoft were virtually unchanged. They were valued around $25 in April 2003 and moved up and down for the next 12 months to finish back near the same level by March 2004. Figure 16.1 details the performance of both Microsoft shares and the Dow Jones Industrial Average over this period, and as you can see, by just selecting one stock you have underperformed the overall market by a staggering 30 per cent. Such an underperformance is almost impossible to make up unless you chase your losses and search out 'riskier' stocks in the hope they will outperform the market next year, which is not a sensible tactic.

In my opinion, only investors who have a particular area of expertise in a stock market sector or individual company should consider participating in such stocks. For the rest of us, there is a far safer and more productive way to invest in the stock market that reduces security risk to a minimum. The best antidote is diversification. With regard to participating in stocks and shares, the best way to diversify your investment is to use a stock market index such as the Standard & Poor's 500 or the Dow Jones Industrials (for the United States), the FTSE 100 (for the United Kingdom), the Nikkei

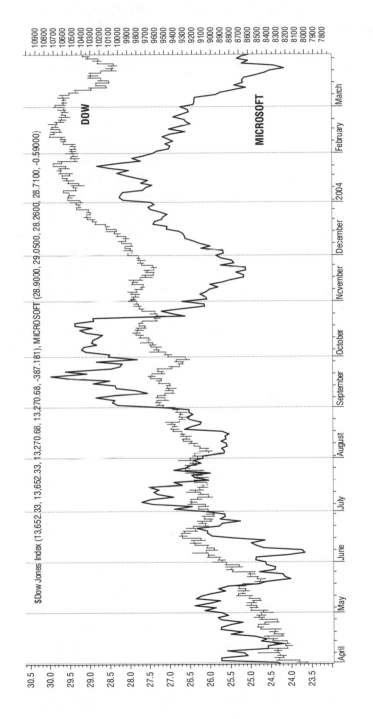

**Figure 16.1** Performance of Microsoft vs Dow Jones Industrial Average, April 2003 to March 2004

225 (for Japan), the Dax 30 (for Germany), the Hang Seng (for Hong Kong) and so on. If you focus your stock market investments on an index, you reduce the negative effect of an underperforming stock or stock market sector, while ensuring that if the overall stock market performs well, you won't miss the ride.

The third hurdle to successful allocation of your investment cash is 'product risk', which is essentially the risk that you could invest your money in a financial product that underperforms its underlying benchmark, thereby cancelling out any benefits you may have enjoyed. For example, imagine the System has signalled that you should invest in the stock market, but you select and invest in a managed fund instead of a tracking instrument and for whatever reason the manager of the fund misses the boat and invests in comparatively poorly performing stocks. At the end of the year, the newspapers are full of headlines about how well the FTSE or Dow has performed, but when you review the performance of the fund you have invested in you find it has failed to make as much money. This is product risk and, unfortunately, it is a more common occurrence than you might think, because such financial products actively managed by fund managers and the like have a poor record when compared to the long-term performance of the general stock market.

There are various statistics flying around about how bad this underperformance actually is, and research by WM Company recently stated that over the last 20 years at least 80 per cent of managed funds couldn't beat the market. Other research puts the percentage somewhat higher, and when you consider that over the years many poorly performing funds would have been closed and therefore their performance removed from the research statistics, the level of underperformance of actively managed products is probably nearer 90 per cent plus. Scary!

Only exceptional managers, such as Anthony Bolton of Fidelity, buck the trend, and unless you're fortunate enough to uncover such a star you are better off placing your cash in a stock market tracker. They have lower fees (typically 0.5 per cent per annum, versus 1.5 per cent or more for a managed fund), minimal managerial input (less risk of human error) and are designed to mirror the performance of their underlying index. You must attempt to limit the effect of product risk, and the most logical route, given that a stock market index generally outperforms the vast majority of fund managers, is to invest in that index.

Applying a market-timing strategy to the performance of a stock market index helps to solve the problems created by market risk, security risk and product risk. It enables you to enjoy the benefits of any current and future bull market trends in stocks and shares without worrying about 'missing the boat'. And, if such trends are not there, then such a strategy should guide you towards placing your money in another asset, namely a safe interest-bearing savings account.

So exactly where should your money go?

# Stock market index timing

Most readers should be familiar with stock market indices and their performance. I'm sure you recall occasions when you've watched the evening news on television or listened to it on the radio and heard references about the performance of the stock market such as 'Today the FTSE closed up 14 points' or 'The Dow closed down 30 points.' These quotes are based upon the returns generated by stock market indices. Each country has its own stock exchange, the overall performance of which is typically measured by the performance of a basket of large capitalized individual stocks, an index. Some nations' stock exchanges have more than one index, covering anything from a basket of stocks from a particular sector right up to almost the entire number of companies traded on the exchange. However, no matter how many indices an exchange may have, they all have a 'flagship' index that you will see quoted in the media. In Great Britain, the index that's regarded as a true barometer of general stock market performance is the FTSE 100 Index; in the United States, there are three indices, the Dow Jones Industrial Average, the Standard & Poor's 500 and the NASDAQ; Germany has the DAX 30; Japan has the Nikkei 225; and so on. Every major nation in the world has its own stock exchange and a quoted stock market index for measuring day-to-day and long-term activity.

Charles H Dow unveiled the first stock market index on 26 May 1896. He wanted to find an easy way for measuring the performance of the US stock market, and although at the time stocks were considered extremely dangerous investments and only suitable for insiders and very savvy operators, Dow's index grew in popularity as the US economy grew and underwent a series of boom-and-bust cycles. His original Dow Jones Industrial Average consisted of just 12 stocks, and he simply added their closing prices together and divided the total by 12. The resulting average figure was published in the *Customer's Afternoon Letter*, a predecessor to the *Wall Street Journal*, and sought to help professionals and amateurs alike to make sense of the daily ups and downs of the stock market.

Charles Dow likened the performance of his index to watching the rising and falling tides of the sea. If the tide was coming in, then each successive push would bring the water closer to the shore, and if the tide was going out, then each successive wave would fall short of the previous one. So it was with the stock market. If the overall long-term trend was upward, then each successive ebb and flow to stock price movements would take the market to new highs, and conversely, if the stock market was in a bear trend, each successive wave of stock index price movement would take the market lower. Higher peaks and troughs in process equalled a bull market (see Figure 16.2) and lower peaks and troughs equated to a bear market (see Figure 16.3).

> Fear tends to manifest itself much more quickly than greed, so volatile markets tend to be on the downside. In up markets, volatility tends to gradually decline.
>
> (Philip Roth)

Although actual market price movements aren't always this uniform, charting the price changes of a stock market index does indeed provide an investor with the most accurate portrayal of the current supply, demand and sentiment of the stock market. Economists, analysts, traders, investors and the media can argue till they're blue in the face about whether the stock market is 'too high' or 'too low', but that is just conjecture. The only true facts are where stock market prices are today and where they have been in the past. A stock market index represents the best way of quickly identifying such information.

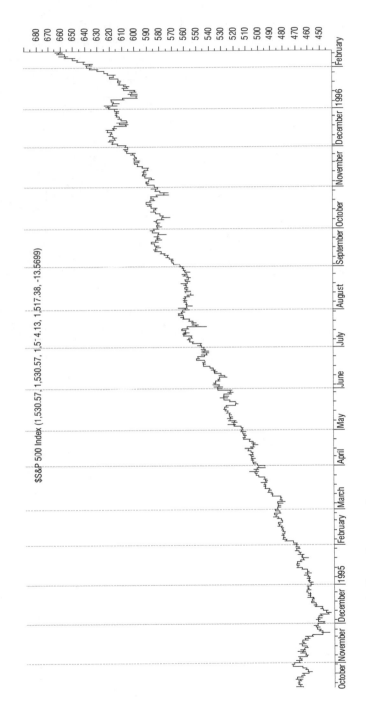

**Figure 16.2**  A bull market trend

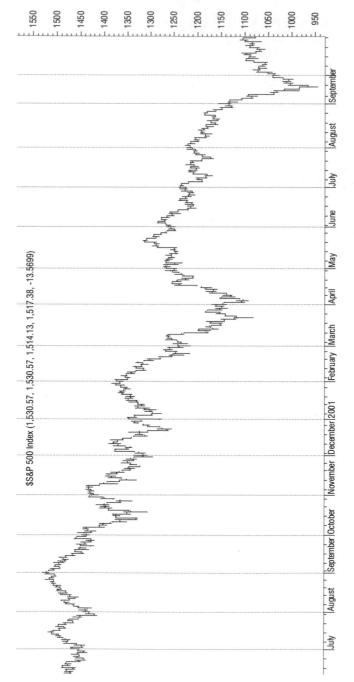

**Figure 16.3**  A bear market trend

As we've just reviewed, to eliminate a number of asset allocation risks, a financial product that bases its own returns upon the performance of a stock market index is particularly useful for the private investor. For example, let's say you have £15,000 to invest and when you begin operating the System it is in 'buy' mode, thereby indicating you should invest in the stock market index you are monitoring. The best and most cost-effective way to invest such an amount of money is via a tracker fund or exchange traded fund (see Appendix B). In the case of a tracker fund, you want one whose performance over the last few years has closely matched that of the underlying stock market index. In addition, it should have comparatively low management fees and allow you instant access to your money when you wish to liquidate your investment. Any competent independent financial adviser should be able to provide you with this information and then help you complete the necessary documentation to invest in the fund.

Once you have invested your cash, your work is complete until the System enters a 'sell' mode. When the System provides a 'sell' signal, your money should be withdrawn from the market and deposited in the highest interest-bearing instant access savings account available at the time. There are a couple of important criteria when selecting a savings account for your money. The first is that you are able to access the cash whenever you wish without any redemption delay or financial penalty, and the second criterion is that the interest rate this account pays should be the most attractive for that type of product. Do not let an adviser recommend a higher-interest-paying product if it means you can't access your money immediately. The purpose of instant access is of course to allow you to reinvest your money into the stock market when the System next signals a 'buy'.

Essentially that's how to operate this stock market index timing option using the Long-Term Investment System. It will always be in either one or the other of two modes, 'buy' (invest in the stock market) or 'sell' (go to cash), and your money should only be in either one or the other of two investments: a stock market index tracking product or an instant access high-interest savings account. Figure 16.4 illustrates the equity profile of a market-timing strategy as it switches from stock market investing to cash (placing money in an interest-bearing savings account).

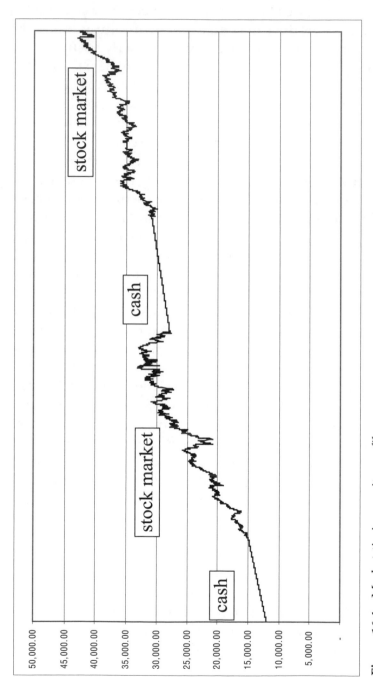

**Figure 16.4** Market-timing equity profile

And remember, the System is an ultra-long-term investment strategy and, because of this, you may remain invested in the stock market or in cash for long periods of time until market conditions change. As always when it comes to speculation, discipline and patience are your strongest attributes.

# Individual stocks and shares or sectors

Another application for the System that may suit more experienced investors who prefer to concentrate on individual stocks or stock market sectors is to use its signals as a filter to indicate whether the overall market is in a bull or a bear trend. If the System is in a 'buy' mode, the logic is that 'a rising tide lifts all boats' and that a bull trend in the overall market is also positive for individual shares and sectors. As well as using the System to measure the overall market condition, you can use it to monitor individual stocks and stock market sectors by simply using their weekly charts rather than the chart of an index. This can create the problem of security risk discussed earlier, and generally I tend to concentrate upon investing in indices. That said, I have, on occasions, used the System to good effect on individual company shares, and one or two notable successes spring to mind: British Airways between July 1991 and August 1994 (up 140 per cent, as shown in Figure 16.5); Sears Roebuck between March 1995 and December 1996 (up 75 per cent, as shown in Figure 16.6); and more recently BHP Billiton from June 2003 to December 2006 (up 200 per cent, as shown in Figure 16.7).

In summary, the Long-Term Investment System can be used as a very effective filter for the condition of the overall market and of market sectors and/or as a timing strategy for individual stocks as well. However, I would caution that, unless you're an experienced investor or have specialist knowledge, you should be wary of participating in individual stocks or stock market sectors, and for the majority of readers I recommend that you concentrate your stock market investing via index tracking products (see Appendix B). And if you need to, consult the services of a recommended independent financial adviser, who can help you select the most appropriate ones.

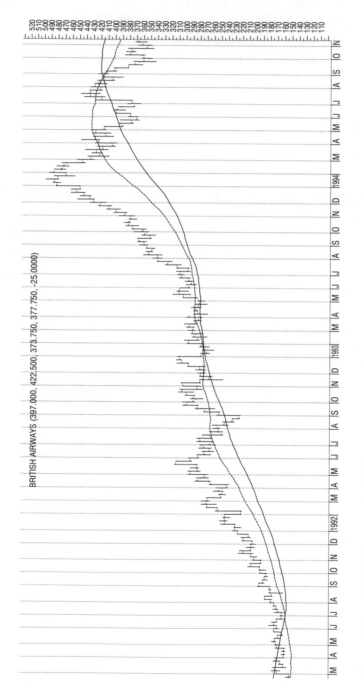

**Figure 16.5**　British Airways, July 1991 to August 1994

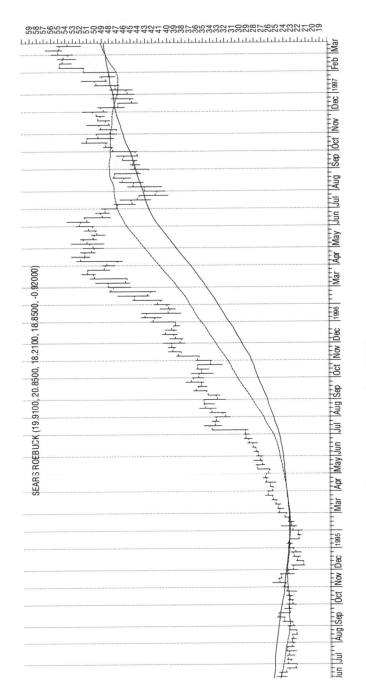

**Figure 16.6** Sear Roebuck, March 1995 to December 1996

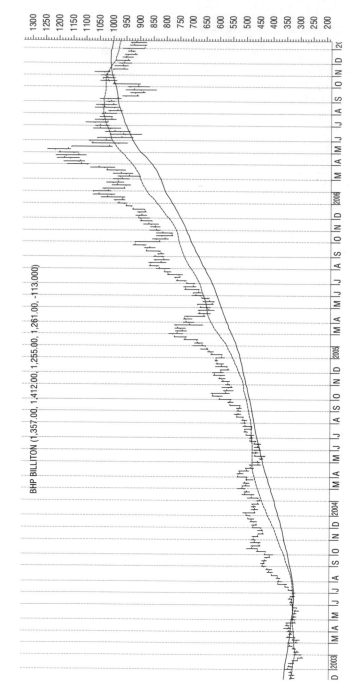

**Figure 16.7** BHP Billiton, June 2003 to December 2006

# How much?

The final aspect of asset allocation is deciding exactly how much money you're prepared to risk on any given investment or strategy. Unfortunately, this is where I'm going to have to sit on the fence because, without detailed knowledge of your current financial condition, your financial goals or your appetite for risk or lack of it, I can't recommend a specific amount. We all have different levels of comfort, and what suits one investor another could consider far too risky. Unless you have the confidence and experience to make such decisions, I would consult a recommended independent financial adviser, who should be able to help you arrive at a figure that suits your financial and risk profile. Certainly, if you have a low appetite for risk, you should invest accordingly, keeping a large percentage of your capital in safer products, or begin with a small amount and gradually build it up as you become more comfortable with investing in the stock market. Better to be safe than sorry.

# 17

# The major stock market indices

When we invest in a stock market index, we are spreading our cash and our risk across a diverse group of highly capitalized companies. While this 'safety in numbers' approach will not result in the spectacular windfall gains sometimes found in individual stocks, it will still benefit from improvements in the economy and also protect you from the risk of having 'all your eggs in one basket'. A major stock market index enables an investor to remain diverse enough to avoid any single stock or stock market sector from causing too much damage and yet sufficiently focused to profit from the successful performance of the leading companies that constitute that index. The following indices are a small but extremely influential selection from the many available to investors around the globe, and they have numerous financial products that monitor and track their performance.

## The Standard & Poor's 500 Composite Index (United States)

The S&P 500 is an index comprising the 500 largest capitalized companies listed on the main US stock exchanges. It is widely considered to be the best indicator of broader stock market performance and includes both 'value' and generally more volatile 'growth' stocks, with the component companies selected by committee in a similar way to the Dow Jones 30 (discussed later). Originally the primary S&P stock market index comprised only 90 companies and was aptly titled the S&P 90. However, in 1957, thanks largely to technical improvements in the calculation of real-time stock prices, the index was expanded to its current size of 500 stocks. The index was originally calculated using the 'market value-weighted method', where a company worth $6 billion is given twice the weighting of a company worth $3 billion; however, in 2005 the index was converted to 'float-weighted', where only the shares of companies that are available for public trading are counted. Despite being considered a bellwether for US economic activity, the index does include a few non-US companies, some of which were formerly US businesses that are now incorporated outside the United States.

FutureSource.com symbol = SP

The 500 companies that make up the index are:

3M Company
Abbott Labs
Abercrombie & Fitch Co
ACE Limited
Adobe Systems
Advanced Micro Devices
AES Corp
Aetna Inc
Affiliated Computer
AFLAC Inc
Agilent Technologies
Air Products & Chemicals
Akamai Technologies Inc
Alcoa Inc
Allegheny Energy
Allegheny Technologies Inc
Allergan Inc
Allied Waste Industries
Allstate Corp
ALLTEL Corp

Altera Corp
Altria Group Inc
Amazon Corp
Ambac Financial Group
Ameren Corporation
American Capital Strategies Ltd
American Electric Power
American Express
American Int'l Group
American Standard
Ameriprise Financial Inc
AmerisourceBergen Corp
Amgen
Anadarko Petroleum
Analog Devices
Anheuser-Busch
Aon Corp
Apache Corp
Apartment Investment & Mgmt
   'A'

Apollo Group
Apple Inc
Applera Corp-Applied
    Biosystems Group
Applied Materials
Archer-Daniels-Midland
Archstone-Smith Trust
Ashland Inc
Assurant Inc
AT&T Inc
Autodesk Inc
Automatic Data Processing Inc
AutoNation Inc
AutoZone Inc
AvalonBay Communities
Avaya Inc
Avery Dennison Corp
Avon Products
Baker Hughes
Ball Corp
Bank of America Corp
Bank of New York Mellon Corp
    (New)
Bard (CR) Inc
Barr Pharmaceuticals Inc
Bausch & Lomb
Baxter International Inc
BB&T Corporation
Bear Stearns Cos
Becton Dickinson
Bed Bath & Beyond
Bemis Company
Best Buy Co Inc
Big Lots Inc
BIOGEN IDEC Inc
BJ Services
Black & Decker Corp
Block H&R
BMC Software

Boeing Company
Boston Properties
Boston Scientific
Bristol-Myers Squibb
Broadcom Corporation
Brown-Forman Corp
Brunswick Corp
Burlington Northern Santa Fe C
CA Inc
Campbell Soup
Capital One Financial
Cardinal Health Inc
Carnival Corp
Caterpillar Inc
CB Richard Ellis Group
CBS Corp
Celgene Corp
CenterPoint Energy
Centex Corp
Century Telephone
Charles Schwab
Chesapeake Energy
Chevron Corp
CH Robinson Worldwide
Chubb Corp
Ciena Corp
CIGNA Corp
Cincinnati Financial
Cintas Corporation
Circuit City Group
Cisco Systems
CIT Group
Citigroup Inc
Citizens Communications
Citrix Systems
Clear Channel Communications
Clorox Co
CME Group Inc
CMS Energy

Coach Inc
Coca Cola Co
Coca-Cola Enterprises
Cognizant Technology Solutions
Colgate-Palmolive
Comcast Corp
Comerica Inc
Commerce Bancorp
Compass Bancshares
Computer Sciences Corp
Compuware Corp
ConAgra Foods Inc
ConocoPhillips
CONSOL Energy Inc
Consolidated Edison
Constellation Brands
Constellation Energy Group
Convergys Corp
Cooper Industries Ltd
Corning Inc
Costco Co
Countrywide Financial Corp
Coventry Health Care Inc
Covidien Ltd
CSX Corp
Cummins Inc
CVS Caremark Corp
Danaher Corp
Darden Restaurants
Dean Foods
Deere & Co
Dell Inc
Developers Diversified Rlty
Devon Energy Corp
Dillard Inc
DIRECTV Group Inc
Discover Financial Services
Dominion Resources
Donnelley (RR) & Sons

Dover Corp
Dow Chemical
Dow Jones & Co
DR Horton
DTE Energy Co
Du Pont (EI)
Duke Energy
Dynegy Inc
E*Trade Financial Corp
Eastman Chemical
Eastman Kodak
Eaton Corp
eBay Inc
Ecolab Inc
Edison Int'l
El Paso Corp
Electronic Arts
Electronic Data Systems
Embarq Corporation
EMC Corp
Emerson Electric
ENSCO Int'l
Entergy Corp
EOG Resources
Equifax Inc
Equity Residential
Estee Lauder Cos
Exelon Corp
Express Scripts
Exxon Mobil Corp
Family Dollar Stores
Fannie Mae
Federal Home Loan Mtg
Federated Investors Inc
FedEx Corporation
Fidelity National Information
  Services
Fifth Third Bancorp
First Data

First Horizon National
FirstEnergy Corp
FIserv Inc
Fluor Corp (New)
Ford Motor
Forest Laboratories
Fortune Brands Inc
FPL Group
Franklin Resources
Freeport-McMoran Cp & Gld
Gannett Co
Gap (The)
General Dynamics
General Electric
General Mills
General Motors
Genl Growth Properties
Genuine Parts
Genworth Financial Inc
Genzyme Corp
Gilead Sciences
Goldman Sachs Group
Goodrich Corporation
Goodyear Tire & Rubber
Google Inc
Grainger (WW) Inc
Halliburton Co
Harley-Davidson
Harman Int'l Industries
Harrah's Entertainment
Hartford Financial SvcGp
Hasbro Inc
Heinz (HJ)
Hercules Inc
Hess Corporation
Hewlett-Packard
Hilton Hotels
Home Depot
Honeywell Int'l Inc

Hospira Inc
Host Hotels & Resorts
Hudson City Bancorp
Humana Inc
Huntington Bancshares
IAC/InterActive Corp
Illinois Tool Works
IMS Health Inc
Ingersoll-Rand Co Ltd
Integrys Energy Group Inc
Intel Corp
International Bus Machines
International Flav/Frag
International Game
   Technology
International Paper
Interpublic Group
Intuit Inc
ITT Corporation
Jabil Circuit
Janus Capital Group
JDS Uniphase Corp
Johnson & Johnson
Johnson Controls
Jones Apparel Group
JPMorgan Chase & Co
Juniper Networks
KB Home
Kellogg Co
KeyCorp
Keyspan Energy
Kimberly-Clark
Kimco Realty
King Pharmaceuticals
KLA-Tencor Corp
Kohl's Corp.
Kraft Foods Inc-A
Kroger Co
L-3 Communications Holdings

Laboratory Corp of America
   Holding
Legg Mason
Leggett & Platt
Lehman Bros
Lennar Corp
Lexmark Int'l Inc
Lilly (Eli) & Co
Limited Brands Inc
Lincoln National
Linear Technology Corp
Liz Claiborne Inc
Lockheed Martin Corp
Loews Corp
Lowe's Cos
LSI Corporation
M&T Bank Corp
Macy's Inc
Manor Care Inc
Marathon Oil Corp
Marriott Int'l
Marsh & McLennan
Marshall & Ilsley Corp
Masco Corp
Mattel Inc
Maxim Integrated Prod
MBIA Inc
McCormick & Co
McDonald's Corp
McGraw-Hill
McKesson Corp (New)
MeadWestvaco Corporation
Medco Health Solutions Inc
Medtronic Inc
MEMC Electronic Materials
Merck & Co
Meredith Corp
Merrill Lynch
MetLife Inc

MGIC Investment
Micron Technology
Microsoft Corp
Millipore Corp
Molex Inc
Molson Coors Brewing
   Company
Monsanto Co
Monster Worldwide
Moody's Corp
Morgan Stanley
Motorola Inc
Murphy Oil
Mylan Laboratories
Nabors Industries Ltd
National City Corp
National Oilwell Varco Inc
National Semiconductor
NCR Corp
Network Appliance
New York Times Cl A
Newell Rubbermaid Co
Newmont Mining Corp (Hldg
   Co)
News Corporation
NICOR Inc
NIKE Inc
NiSource Inc
Noble Corporation
Nordstrom
Norfolk Southern Corp
Northern Trust Corp
Northrop Grumman Corp
Novell Inc
Novellus Systems
Nucor Corp
NVIDIA Corp
Occidental Petroleum
Office Depot

OfficeMax Inc
Omnicom Group
Oracle Corp
PACCAR Inc
Pactiv Corp
Pall Corp
Parker-Hannifin
Patterson Cos Inc
Paychex Inc
Peabody Energy
Penney (JC)
Pepsi Bottling Group
PepsiCo Inc
PerkinElmer
Pfizer Inc
PG&E Corp
Pinnacle West Capital
Pitney-Bowes
Plum Creek Timber Co
PNC Financial Services
Polo Ralph Lauren Corp
PPG Industries
PPL Corp
Praxair Inc
Precision Castparts
Principal Financial Group
Procter & Gamble
Progress Energy Inc
Progressive Corp
ProLogis
Prudential Financial
Public Serv Enterprise Inc
Public Storage
Pulte Homes Inc
QLogic Corp
QUALCOMM Inc
Quest Diagnostics
Questar Corp
Qwest Communications Int

RadioShack Corp
Raytheon Co (New)
Regions Financial Corp
Reynolds American Inc
Robert Half International
Rockwell Automation Inc
Rockwell Collins
Rohm & Haas
Rowan Cos
Ryder System
SAFECO Corp
Safeway Inc
SanDisk Corporation
Sara Lee Corp
Schering-Plough
Schlumberger Ltd
Scripps (EW) 'A'
Sealed Air Corp (New)
Sears Holdings Corporation
Sempra Energy
Sherwin-Williams
Sigma-Aldrich
Simon Property Group Inc
SLM Corporation
Smith International
Snap-On Inc
Solectron
Southern Co
Southwest Airlines
Sovereign Bancorp
Spectra Energy Corp
Sprint Nextel Corp
St Jude Medical
Stanley Works
Staples Inc
Starbucks Corp
Starwood Hotels & Resorts
State Street Corp
Stryker Corp

Sun Microsystems
Sunoco Inc
SunTrust Banks
Supervalu Inc
Symantec Corp
Synovus Financial
Sysco Corp
T Rowe Price Group
Target Corp
TECO Energy
Tektronix Inc
Tellabs Inc
Temple-Inland
Tenet Healthcare Corp
Teradyne Inc
Terex Corp
Texas Instruments
Textron Inc
The Hershey Company
The Travelers Companies Inc
Thermo Fisher Scientific
Tiffany & Co
Time Warner Inc
TJX Companies Inc
Torchmark Corp
Transocean Inc
Tribune Co
TXU Corp
Tyco Electronics Ltd
Tyco International (New)
Tyson Foods
US Bancorp
Union Pacific
Unisys Corp
United Health Group Inc
United Parcel Service
United States Steel Corp
United Technologies
Unum Group

UST Inc
Valero Energy
Varian Medical Systems
Verisign Inc
Verizon Communications
VF Corp
Viacom Inc (New)
Vornado Realty Trust
Vulcan Materials
Wachovia Corp (New)
Wal-Mart Stores
Walgreen Co
Walt Disney Co
Washington Mutual
Waste Management Inc
Waters Corporation
Watson Pharmaceuticals
Weatherford International Ltd
WellPoint Inc
Wells Fargo
Wendy's International
Western Union Co
Weyerhauser Corp
Whirlpool Corp
Whole Foods Market
Williams Cos
Windstream Corporation
Wrigley (Wm) Jr
Wyeth
Wyndham Worldwide
XL Capital
XTO Energy Inc
Xcel Energy Inc
Xerox Corp
Xilinx Inc
Yahoo Inc
Yum! Brands Inc
Zimmer Holdings
Zions Bancorp

# The Dow Jones Industrial Average (United States)

Also referred to as the DJIA, Dow 30 or simply the Dow, it is an index consisting of the 30 largest capitalized and most widely held companies in the United States. Do not be misled by the 'industrial' reference in the title, as this is largely historical and nowadays many of the constituent companies have little exposure to heavy industry. Originally the concept of Charles Dow, the index was first published way back in 1896, when it comprised just 12 companies. In 1916, the number of stocks was increased to 20 and finally, in 1928, just before the big stock market crash of 1929, the index was increased again to its current level of 30 companies. The index is calculated as a 'scaled average', which involves taking the sum of the component stocks and dividing them by a 'divisor' to generate the value of the index. This method of calculation seeks to compensate for the effect of stock splits and other adjustments. Although usually more quoted in the media than the S&P 500, the Dow Jones Industrial Average is considered by many professionals to be less of a true measure of US corporate activity and performance, owing to the limited number of companies in the index.

FutureSource.com symbol = DJY

The 30 companies that make up the index are:

3M
Alcoa
Altria Group
American Express
American International Group
AT&T
Boeing
Caterpillar
Citigroup
Coca-Cola
DuPont
ExxonMobil

General Electric
General Motors
Hewlett-Packard
Home Depot
Honeywell
Intel
IBM
Johnson & Johnson
JP Morgan Chase
McDonald's
Merck
Microsoft

Pfizer

Procter & Gamble

United Technologies Corporation

Verizon Communications

Wal-Mart

Walt Disney

# The NASDAQ-100 Index (United States)

The National Association of Securities Dealers Automated Quotations system (NASDAQ), to give it its full title, is the largest screen-based electronic exchange in the United States and widely considered to be a barometer of the technology industry. With over 3,000 constituents, it lists more companies and trades more shares per day than any other US market, and although it began trading in 1971, it wasn't until the dotcom boom of the 1990s that the index really came to the fore. The NASDAQ-100 Index, which began life in 1985, is a modified capital-weighted index designed to track the performance of the 100 largest and most actively traded non-financial domestic and international stocks listed on the NASDAQ.

FutureSource.com symbol = NQ

The 100 companies that make up the index are:

Activision Inc

Adobe Systems Incorporated

Akamai Technologies Inc

Altera Corporation

Amazon.com Inc

Amgen Inc

Amylin Pharmaceuticals

Apollo Group Inc

Apple Inc

Applied Materials Inc

Autodesk Inc

BEA Systems Inc

Bed Bath & Beyond Inc

Biogen Idec Inc

Broadcom Corporation

Cadence Design Systems

CDW Corporation

Celgene Corporation

Cephalon Inc

Check Point Software

   Technologies Ltd

CheckFree Corporation

CH Robinson Worldwide Inc

Cintas Corporation

Cisco Systems Inc

Citrix Systems Inc

Cognizant Technology Solutions

   Corporation

Comcast Corporation

Costco Wholesale Corporation

Dell Inc

DENTSPLY International Inc

Discovery Holding Co
eBay Inc
Echostar Communications
    Corporation
Electronic Arts Inc
Expedia Inc
Expeditors International of
    Washington Inc
Express Scripts Inc
Fastenal Company
Fiserv Inc
Flextronics International Ltd
Foster Wheeler Corporation
Garmin Ltd
Genzyme Corporation
Gilead Sciences Inc
Google Inc
IAC/InterActiveCorp
Infosys Technologies
Intel Corporation
Intuit Inc
Intuitive Surgical Inc
Joy Global Inc
Juniper Networks Inc
KLA-Tencor Corporation
Lam Research Corporation
Lamar Advertising Company
Level 3 Communications
Liberty Global Inc
Liberty Media Corporation,
    Interactive Series A
Linear Technology Corporation
LM Ericsson Telephone
    Company
Logitech International SA
Marvell Technology Group Ltd
Maxim Integrated Products Inc
Microchip Technology
    Incorporated

Microsoft Corporation
Millicom International Cellular
    SA
Monster Worldwide Inc
Network Appliance Inc
NII Holdings Inc
NTL Incorporated
NVIDIA Corporation
Oracle Corporation
PACCAR Inc
Patterson Companies Inc
Patterson-UTI Energy Inc
Paychex Inc
PetSmart Inc
QUALCOMM Incorporated
Research in Motion Limited
Ross Stores Inc
Ryanair Holdings PLC
SanDisk Corporation
Sears Holdings Corporation
Sepracor Inc
Sigma-Aldrich Corporation
Sirius Satellite Radio Inc
Staples Inc
Starbucks Corporation
Sun Microsystems Inc
Symantec Corporation
Tellabs Inc
Teva Pharmaceutical Industries
    Limited
UAL Corporation
VeriSign Inc
Vertex Pharmaceuticals
Whole Foods Market Inc
Wynn Resorts Ltd
Xilinx Inc
XM Satellite Radio Holdings Inc
Yahoo! Inc

# The FTSE 100 Index (United Kingdom)

The FTSE 100 is an index comprising the 100 largest capitalized companies in England, Wales, Scotland and Northern Ireland. The constituents of the index are determined quarterly by their market capitalization, and the performance of the 'Footsie', to use its popular name, is widely viewed as the barometer for economic and corporate performance in the United Kingdom. Other related indices are: the FTSE 250 Index, which covers the next largest 250 companies; the FTSE 350 Index, which aggregates the FTSE 100 and FTSE 250 indices; the FTSE SmallCap Index, which as the name suggests covers publicly traded companies with a relatively smaller market capitalization; and the FTSE All-Share Index, which aggregates the FTSE 100, FTSE 250 and FTSE SmallCap indices. All of these indices provide useful information regarding the performance of corporate Britain, but it's the FTSE 100 Index that is most widely quoted in the media.

FutureSource.com symbol = LFT

The 100 companies that make up the index are:

| | |
|---|---|
| 3i | BT Group |
| Alliance & Leicester | Cable & Wireless |
| Alliance Boots | Cadbury Schweppes |
| Anglo American | Capita Group |
| Antofagasta | Carnival |
| Associated British Foods | Centrica |
| AstraZeneca | Compass Group |
| Aviva | Daily Mail and General Trust |
| BAE Systems | Diageo |
| Barclays Bank | Drax Group |
| Barratt Developments | DSG International |
| BG Group | Enterprise Inns |
| BHP Billiton | Experian |
| BP | Friends Provident |
| British Airways | GlaxoSmithKline |
| British American Tobacco | Hammerson |
| British Land Company | Hanson |
| British Sky Broadcasting Group | HBOS |

Home Retail Group
HSBC
ICAP
Imperial Chemical Industries
Imperial Tobacco
InterContinental Hotels Group
International Power
Invesco
ITV
J Sainsbury
Johnson Matthey
Kazakhmys
Kelda Group
Kingfisher
Land Securities Group
Legal & General
Liberty International
Lloyds TSB
Lonmin
Man Group
Marks & Spencer
Mitchells & Butlers
Morrison (Wm) Supermarkets
National Grid
Next
Northern Rock
Old Mutual
Pearson
Persimmon
Prudential
Punch Taverns
Reckitt Benckiser

Reed Elsevier
Resolution
Reuters Group
Rexam
Rio Tinto Group
Rolls-Royce Group
Royal & Sun Alliance Insurance
Royal Bank of Scotland Group
Royal Dutch Shell
SABMiller
Sage Group
Schroders
Scottish & Newcastle
Scottish & Southern Energy
Severn Trent
Shire Pharmaceuticals Group
Slough Estates
Smith & Nephew
Smiths Group
Standard Chartered bank
Standard Life
Tate & Lyle
Tesco
Unilever
United Utilities
Vedanta Resources
Vodaphone
Whitbread
Wolseley
WPP Group
Xstrata
Yell Group

# The DAX 30 Index (Germany)

The Deutsche Aktien Xchange 30 is an index comprising the 30 largest companies on the Frankfurt Stock Exchange. Unusually it is a total return index, which means it includes the dividends paid by its constituent companies as well as the changes in their share prices. The DAX is known by many professionals as an 'exporters' index', owing to the fact that so many German products are sold overseas, as can be seen in the popularity of BMW, Mercedes and Volkswagen cars in China and India.

FutureSource.com symbol = DAX

The 30 companies that make up the index are:

| | |
|---|---|
| Adidas AG | Fresenius Medical Care |
| Allianz | Henkel |
| BASF | Hypo Real Estate |
| Bayer AG | Infineon Technologies |
| BMW | Linde AG |
| Commerzbank | MAN |
| Continental AG | Merck |
| DaimlerChrysler | METRO |
| Deutsche Bank | Munich Re |
| Deutsche Börse | RWE |
| Deutsche Lufthansa | SAP |
| Deutsche Post | Siemens |
| Deutsche Postbank | ThyssenKrupp |
| Deutsche Telekom | TUI |
| E.ON | Volkswagen (VW) |

# The CAC 40 Index (France)

The Cotation Assistée en Continu (Continuous Assisted Quotation) 40 is a capital-weighted index comprising the 40 most significant companies listed on the Paris Bourse. Unusually its component companies have a high percentage of foreign ownership (approximately 45 per cent), illustrating the multinational nature of large French businesses.

FutureSource.com symbol = GMCT

The 40 companies that make up the index are:

| | |
|---|---|
| Accor | Lafarge |
| Air France-KLM | Lagardère |
| Air Liquide | LVMH |
| Alcatel-Lucent | Michelin |
| Alstom | Pernod Ricard |
| Arcelor Mittal | PPR |
| AXA | PSA Peugeot Citroën |
| BNP Paribas | Renault |
| Bouygues | Saint-Gobain |
| Capgemini | Sanofi-Aventis |
| Carrefour | Schneider Electric |
| Crédit Agricole | Société Générale |
| Dexia | STMicroelectronics |
| EADS | SUEZ |
| EDF | Total |
| Essilor | Unibail-Rodamco |
| France Telecom | Vallourec |
| Gaz de France | Veolia Environnement |
| Groupe Danone | VINCI |
| L'Oréal | Vivendi |

# The Nikkei 225 Index (Japan)

The Nikkei 225 is an index consisting of the largest capitalized companies in Japan and is the most widely quoted index of Asian stocks. It is a price-weighted average, with its constituent companies reviewed on an annual basis and the daily price movements calculated by the *Nihon Keizai Shimbun* (*Nikkei*) newspaper. Many readers might feel they wouldn't be very familiar with the components of the Nikkei, but I'm sure most of us are aware of the products from Bridgestone, Casio, Toshiba, Sanyo, Kawasaki, Mazda, Sony, Pioneer, Fuji, Sharp, Nikon, Honda, Toyota and Yamaha, to name but a few. The overseas success of such companies makes the Nikkei an important global stock market index.

FutureSource.com symbol = NK

The 225 companies that make up the index are:

Advantest Corp
Aeon Co Ltd
Ajinomoto Co Inc
All Nippon Airways Co Ltd
Alps Electric Co Ltd
Asahi Breweries Ltd
Asahi Glass Co Ltd
Asahi Kasei Corp
Astellas Pharma Inc
Bridgestone Corp
Canon Inc
Casio Computer Co Ltd
Chiyoda Corp
Chubu Electric Power Co Inc
Chugai Pharmaceutical Co Ltd
Citizen Holdings Co Ltd
Clarion Co Ltd
Comsys Holdings Corp
Credit Saison Co Ltd
CSK Holdings Corp
Daiichi Sankyo Co Ltd
Daikin Industries Ltd
Dai Nippon Printing Co Ltd
Dainippon Sumitomo Pharma
 Co Ltd
Daiwa House Industry Co Ltd
Daiwa Securities Group Inc
Denki Kagaku Kogyo KK
Denso Corp
Dentsu Inc
DOWA Holdings Co Ltd
Ebara Corp
Eisai Co Ltd
East Japan Railway Co
Fanuc Ltd
Fast Retailing Co Ltd
Fuji Electric Holdings Co Ltd
Fujifilm Holdings Corp
Fuji Heavy Industries Ltd

Fujikura Ltd
Fujitsu Ltd
Furukawa Co Ltd
GS Yuasa Corp
Heiwa Real Estate Co Ltd
Hino Motors Ltd
Hitachi Ltd
Hitachi Zosen Corp
Hokuetsu Paper Mills Ltd
Honda Motor Co Ltd
IHI Corp
Inpex Holdings Inc
Isetan Co Ltd
Isuzi Motors Ltd
Itochu Corp
Japan Airlines Corp
Japan Tobacco Inc
JFE Holdings Inc
JGC Corp
JTEKT Corp
Kajima Corp
Kao Corp
Kawasaki Heavy Industries Ltd
Kawasaki Kisen Kaisha Ltd
KDDI Corp
Keio Corp
Keisei Electric Railway Co Ltd
Kikkoman Corp
Kirin Holdings Co Ltd
Kobe Steel Ltd
Komatsu Ltd
Konami Corp
Konica Minolta Holdings Inc
Kubota Corp
Kumagai Gumi Co Ltd
Kuraray Co Ltd
Kyocera Corp
Kyowa Hakko Kogyo Co Ltd
Marubeni Corp

Marui Co Ltd
Matsushita Electric Industrial
  Co Ltd
Matsushita Electric Works Ltd
Mazda Motor Corp
Meidensha Corp
Meiji Dairies Corp
Meiji Seika Kaisha Ltd
Millea Holdings Inc
Minebea Co Ltd
Mitsubishi Corp
Mitsubishi Chemical Holdings
  Corp
Mitsubishi Electric Corp
Mitsubishi Estate Co Ltd
Mitsubishi Heavy Industries Ltd
Mitsubishi Logistics Corp
Mitsubishi Materials Corp
Mitsubishi Motors Corp
Mitsubishi Paper Mills Ltd
Mitsubishi Rayon Co Ltd
Mitsubishi UFJ Financial Group
  Inc
Mitsubishi UFJ Nicos Co Ltd
Mitsui & Co Ltd
Mitsui Chemicals Inc
Mitsui Engineering &
  Shipbuilding Co Ltd
Mitsui Fudosan Co Ltd
Mitsui Mining and Smelting Co
  Ltd
Mitsui OSK Lines Ltd
Mitsui Sumitomo Insurance Co
  Ltd
Mitsui Trust Holdings Inc
Mitsukoshi Ltd
Mitsumi Electric Co Ltd
Mizuho Financial Group Inc

Mizuho Trust & Banking Co Ltd
NEC Corp
NGK Insulators Ltd
Nichirei Corp
Nikko Cordial Corp
Nikon Corp
Nippon Express Co Ltd
Nippon Kayaku Co Ltd
Nippon Light Metal Co Ltd
Nippon Meat Packers Inc
Nippon Mining Holdings Inc
Nippon Oil Corp
Nippon Paper Group Inc
Nippon Sheet Glass Co Ltd
Nippon Soda Co Ltd
Nippon Steel Corp
Nippon Suisan Kaisha Ltd
Nippon Telegraph & Telephone
  Corp
Nippon Yusen KK
Nissan Chemical Industries Ltd
Nissan Motor Co Ltd
Nisshinbo Industries Inc
Nisshin Seifun Group Inc
Nitto Boseki Co Ltd
Nomura Holdings Inc
NSK Ltd
NTN Corp
NTT Data Corp
NTT DoCoMo Inc
Obayashi Corp
Odakyu Electric Railway Co Ltd
Oji Paper Co Ltd
Oki Electric Industry Co Ltd
Okuma Corp
Olympus Corp
Osaka Gas Co Ltd
Pioneer Corp

Resona Holdings Inc
Ricoh Co Ltd
Sanyo Electric Co Ltd
Sapporo Holdings Ltd
Secom Co Ltd
Sekisui House Ltd
Seven & i Holdings Co Ltd
Sharp Corp
Shimizu Corp
Shin-Etsu Chemical Co Ltd
Shinko Securities Co Ltd
Shinsei Bank Ltd
Shionogi & Co Ltd
Shiseido Co Ltd
Showa Denko KK
Showa Shell Sekiyu KK
Sky Perfect JSAT Corp
Softbank Corp
Sojitz Corp
Sompo Japan Insurance Inc
Sony Corp
Sumitomo Corp
Sumitomo Chemical Co Ltd
Sumitomo Electric Industries
   Ltd
Sumitomo Heavy Industries Ltd
Sumitomo Metal Industries Ltd
Sumitomo Metal Mining Co Ltd
Sumitomo Mitsui Financial
   Group Inc
Sumitomo Osaka Cement Co
   Ltd
Sumitomo Realty &
   Development Co Ltd
Suzuki Motor Corp
Taiheiyo Cement Corp
Taisei Corp
Taiyo Yuden Co Ltd

Takara Holdings Inc
Takashimaya Co Ltd
Takeda Pharmaceutical Co Ltd
T&D Holdings Inc
TDK Corp
Teijin Ltd
Terumo Corp
The Bank of Yokohama Ltd
The Chiba Bank Ltd
The Furukawa Electric Co Ltd
The Japan Steel Works Ltd
The Kansai Electric Power Co
   Inc
The Nisshin Oillio Group Ltd
The Shizuoka Bank Ltd
The Sumitomo Trust & Banking
   Co Ltd
The Tokyo Electric Power Co Inc
The Yokohama Rubber Co Ltd
Toagosei Co Ltd
Tobu Railway Co Ltd
Toho Co Ltd
Toho Zinc Co Ltd
Tokai Carbon Co Ltd
Tokyo Dome Corp
Tokyo Electron Ltd
Tokyo Gas Co Ltd
Tokyu Corp
Tokyu Land Corp
Toppan Printing Co Ltd
Topy Industries Ltd
Toray Industries Inc
Toshiba Corp
Tosoh Corp
TOTO Ltd
Toyobo Co Ltd
Toyo Seikan Kaisha Ltd
Toyota Motor Corp

Toyota Tsusho Corp
Trend Micro Inc
Ube Industries Ltd
Unitika Ltd
West Japan Railway Co

Yahoo Japan Corp
Yamaha Corp
Yamato Holdings Co Ltd
Yokogawa Electric Corp

# The Hang Seng Index (Hong Kong)

The Hang Seng is an index comprising the 39 largest capitalized companies in Hong Kong, and it is compiled and maintained by a wholly owned subsidiary of the second-largest bank in Hong Kong, the Hang Seng Bank. The index is becoming widely recognized as a useful way to gain exposure to the growth of the People's Republic of China because, as you can see from the current list of components, a number of major Chinese companies are now listed in the index. With participation in the Chinese market itself still somewhat restricted, the Hang Seng is fast becoming a China proxy for many investors.

FutureSource.com symbol = HHA

The 39 companies that make up the index are:

Bank of China Ltd
Bank of East Asia Ltd
BOC Hong Kong (Holdings) Ltd
Cathay Pacific Airways Ltd
Cheung Kong (Holdings) Ltd
Cheung Kong Infrastructure
    Holdings Ltd
China Construction Bank
China Life
China Merchants Holdings
    (International) Co Ltd
China Mobile (Hong Kong ) Ltd
China Netcom Group
    Corporation (Hong Kong) Ltd
China Resources Enterprise Ltd

China Unicom Ltd
CITIC Pacific Ltd
CLP Holdings Ltd
CNOOC Ltd
COSCO Pacific Ltd
Esprit Holdings Ltd
Foxconn International Holdings
    Ltd
Hang Lung Properties Ltd
Hang Seng Bank Ltd
Henderson Land Development
    Co Ltd
HKEx Limited
Hong Kong and China Gas
    Company Limited

Hong Kong Electric Holdings
  Ltd
HSBC Holdings plc
Hutchison Whampoa Ltd
Industrial and Commercial Bank
  of China
Li & Fung Ltd
MTR Corporation Ltd
New World Development Co
  Ltd

PCCW Ltd
Ping An Insurance
Sino Land Co Ltd
Sinopec Corp
Sun Hung Kai Properties Ltd
Swire Pacific Ltd 'A'
Wharf (Holdings) Ltd
Yue Yuen Industrial (Holdings)
  Ltd

# 18

# The System – historical performance 1951–2007

## S&P 500 Composite Index historical record

*Note:* The performance data for the historical results detailed in this section are based upon cash data of the S&P 500 Composite Index as supplied by Commodity Systems Inc and Equis International Inc.

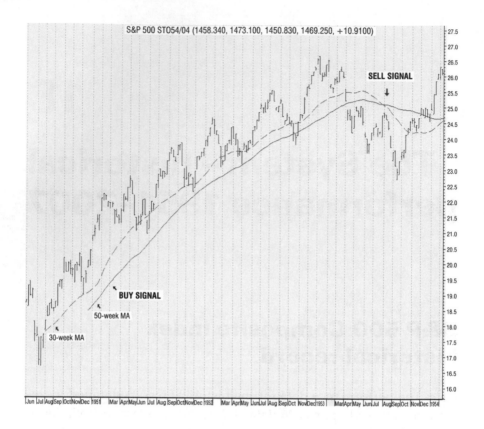

S&P 500 STO54/04 (1458.340, 1473.100, 1450.830, 1469.250, +10.9100)

SELL SIGNAL

BUY SIGNAL

50-week MA

30-week MA

6 January 1951        Opened position @ 20.77
14 August 1953       Closed position @ 24.75        = profit 19.16%

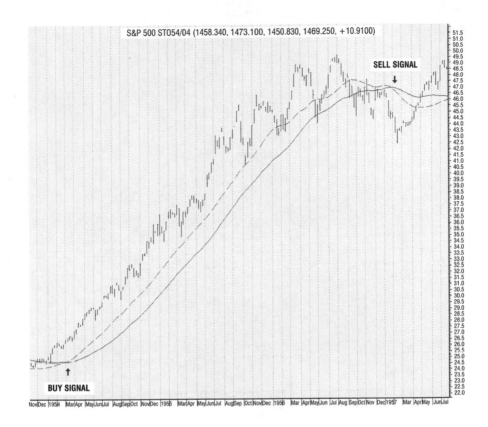

S&P 500 STO54/04 (1458.340, 1473.100, 1450.830, 1469.250, +10.9100)

SELL SIGNAL

BUY SIGNAL

| 5 March 1954 | Opened position @ 26.25 | |
|---|---|---|
| 8 February 1957 | Closed position @ 44.53 | = profit 69.64% |

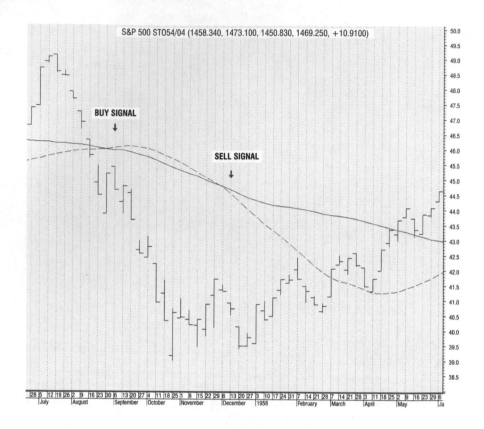

S&P 500 STO54/04 (1458.340, 1473.100, 1450.830, 1469.250, +10.9100)

BUY SIGNAL

SELL SIGNAL

6 September 1957     Opened position @ 45.44

13 December 1957     Closed position @ 40.92       = (loss 9.95%)

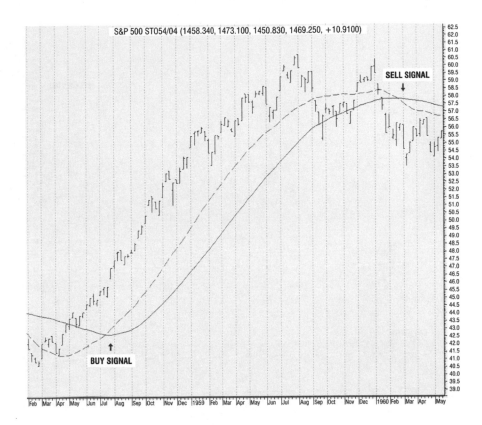

S&P 500 ST054/04 (1458.340, 1473.100, 1450.830, 1469.250, +10.9100)

25 July 1958      Opened position @ 46.33

4 March 1960      Closed position @ 56.12      = profit 21.13%

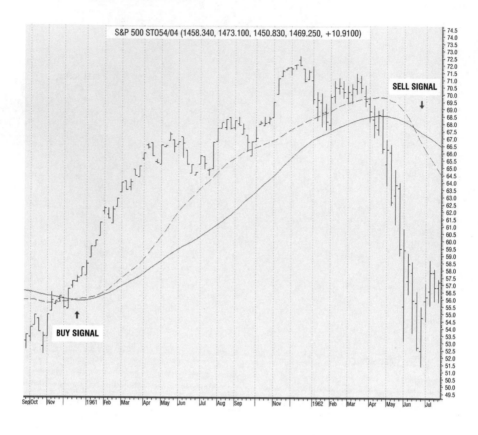

| 30 December 1960 | Opened position @ 57.52 | |
| 29 June 1962 | Closed position @ 52.45 | = (loss 8.81%) |

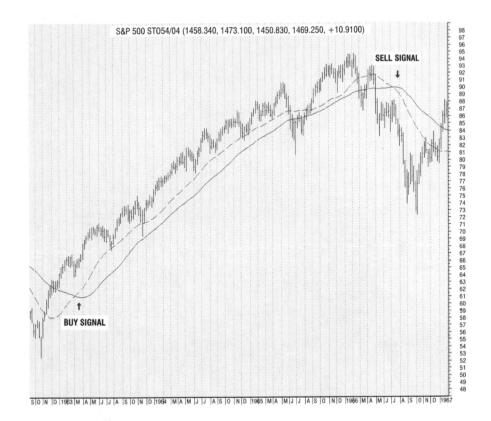

S&P 500 STO54/04 (1458.340, 1473.100, 1450.830, 1469.250, +10.9100)

SELL SIGNAL

BUY SIGNAL

| 15 March 1963 | Opened position @ 65.51 | |
|---|---|---|
| 22 July 1966 | Closed position @ 86.99 | = profit 32.79% |

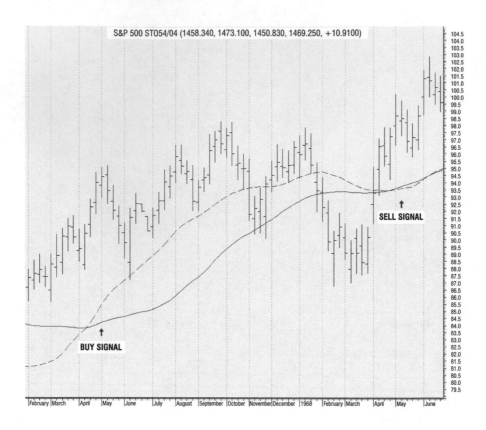

| 28 April 1967 | Opened position @ 92.62 | |
| 10 May 1968 | Closed position @ 98.35 | = profit 6.19% |

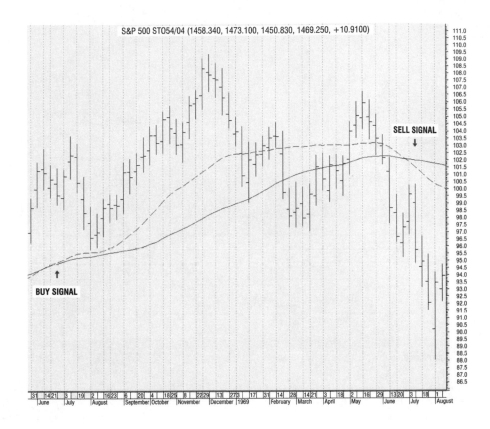

S&P 500 STO54/04 (1458.340, 1473.100, 1450.830, 1469.250, +10.9100)

| | | |
|---|---|---|
| 21 June 1968 | Opened position @ 100.13 | |
| 11 July 1969 | Closed position @ 99.03 | = (loss 1.10%) |

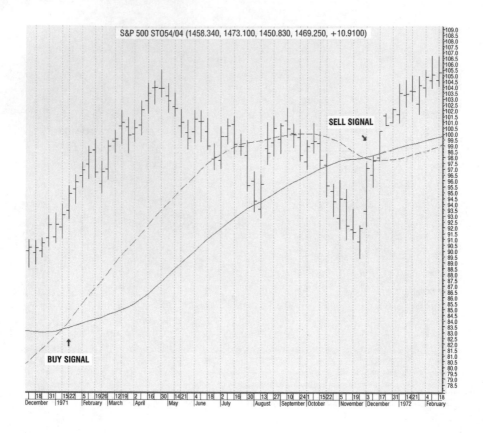

S&P 500 STO54/04 (1458.340, 1473.100, 1450.830, 1469.250, +10.9100)

| 29 January 1971 | Opened position @ 95.28 | |
| 10 December 1971 | Closed position @ 96.51 | = profit 1.29% |

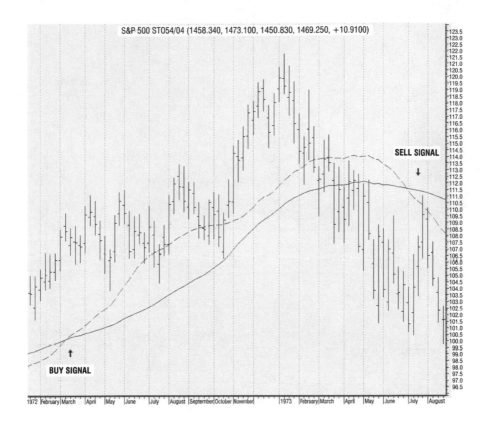

S&P 500 ST054/04 (1458.340, 1473.100, 1450.830, 1469.250, +10.9100)

**SELL SIGNAL**

**BUY SIGNAL**

24 March 1972      Opened position @ 107.59
13 July 1973       Closed position @ 102.14        – (loss 5.07%)

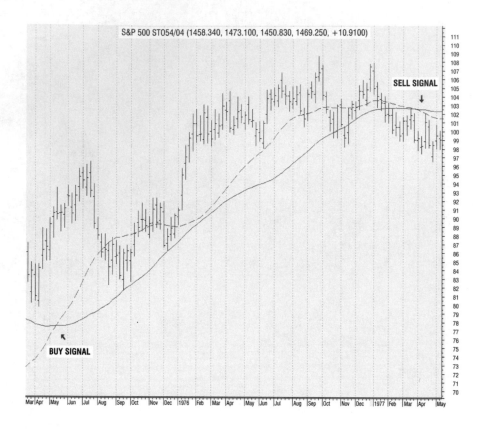

S&P 500 ST054/04 (1458.340, 1473.100, 1450.830, 1469.250, +10.9100)

SELL SIGNAL

BUY SIGNAL

23 May 1975        Opened position @ 90.53

7 April 1977         Closed position @ 98.23      = profit 8.51%

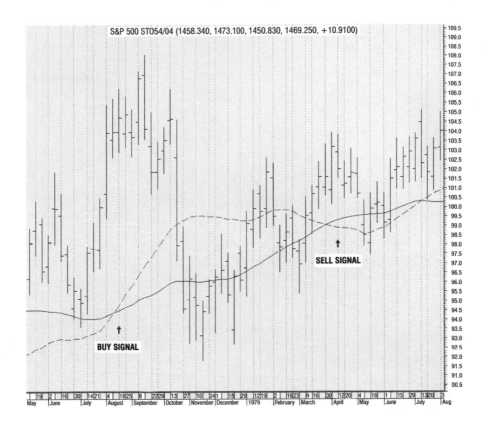

| | |
|---|---|
| 25 August 1978 | Opened position @ 103.89 |
| 12 April 1979 | Closed position @ 102.87    = (loss 0.98%) |

27 July 1979          Opened position @ 101.59
21 August 1981        Closed position @ 131.66        = profit 29.60%

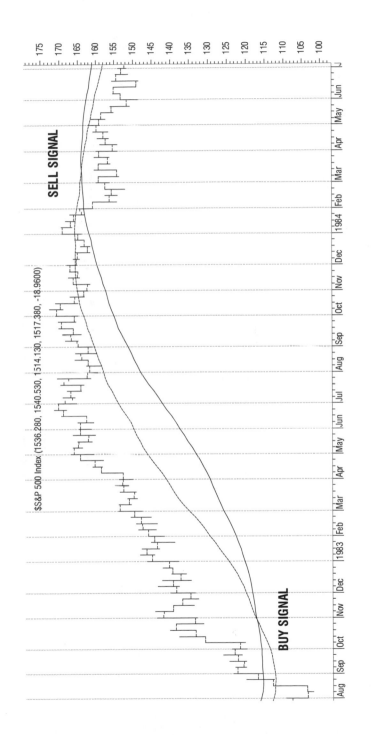

$S\&P 500 Index (1536.280, 1540.530, 1514.130, 1517.380, -18.9600)

**SELL SIGNAL**

**BUY SIGNAL**

12 November 1982   Opened position @ 142.12
23 March 1984     Closed position @ 159.18    = profit 12.00%

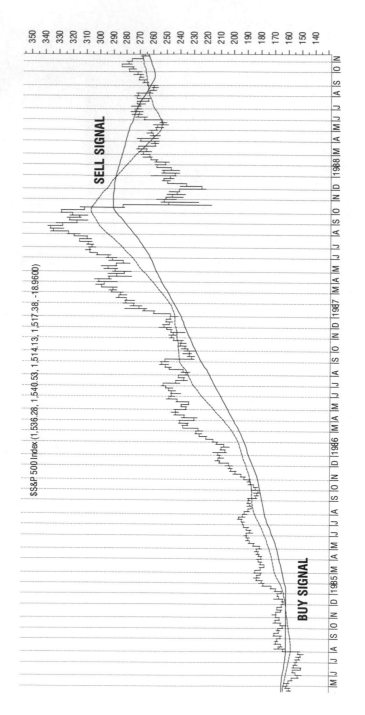

$S&P 500 Index (1,536.28, 1,540.53, 1,514.13, 1,517.38, -18.9600)

**SELL SIGNAL**

**BUY SIGNAL**

350 340 330 320 310 300 290 280 270 260 250 240 230 220 210 200 190 180 170 160 150 140

M J J A S O N D 1985 M A M J J A S O N D 1986 M A M J J A S O N D 1987 M A M J J A S O N D 1988 M A M J J A S O N

30 November 1984    Opened position @ 166.90
15 January 1988      Closed position @ 243.46        = profit 45.87%

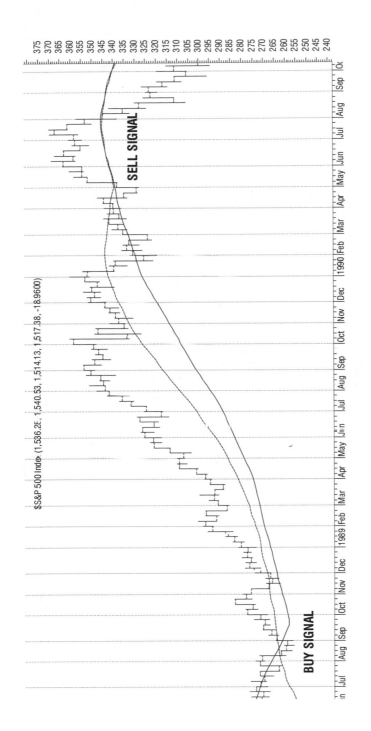

$S&P 500 Index (1,536.2E, 1,540.53, 1,514.13, 1,517.38, -18.9600)

BUY SIGNAL

SELL SIGNAL

2 September 1988     Opened position @ 259.69
29 June 1990        Closed position @ 355.43        = profit 36.87%

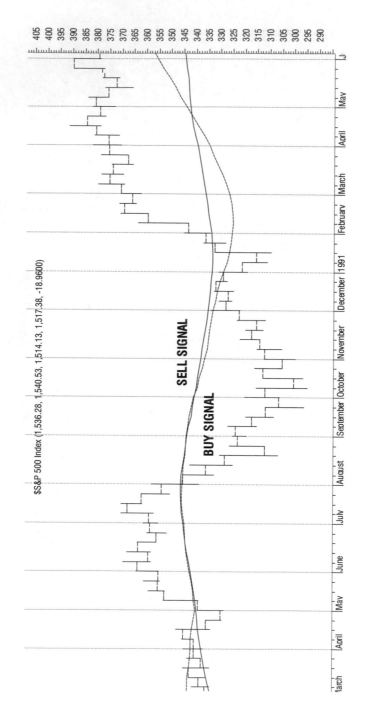

$S&P 500 Index (1,536.28, 1,540.53, 1,514.13, 1,517.38, -18.9600)

SELL SIGNAL

BUY SIGNAL

7 September 1990    Opened position @ 322.56

19 October 1990    Closed position @ 300.03    = (loss 6.98%)

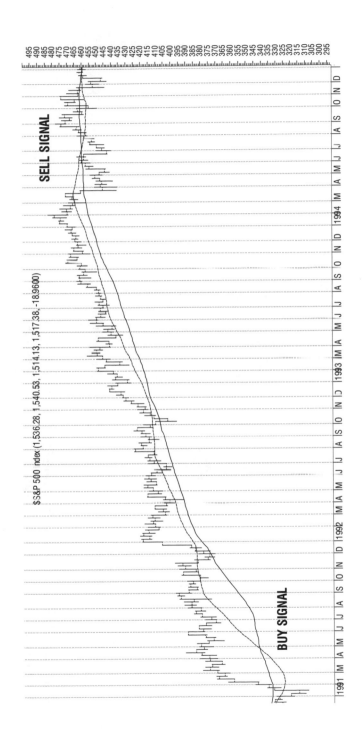

10 May 1991      Opened position @ 380.78

15 July 1994      Closed position @ 449.56      = profit 18.06%

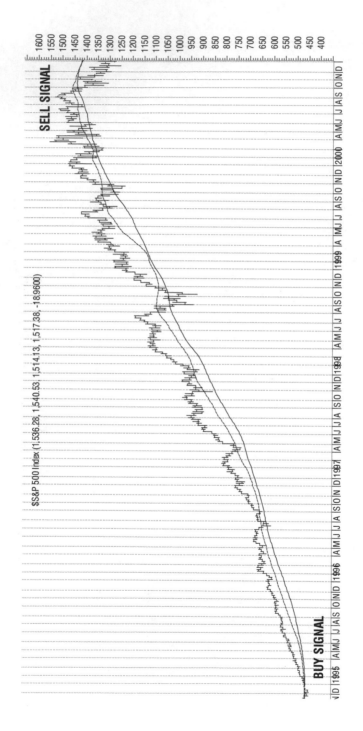

SELL SIGNAL

$S&P 500 Index (1,536.28, 1,540.53, 1,514.13, 1,517.38, -18.9600)

BUY SIGNAL

6 January 1995    Opened position @ 459.21
5 January 2001    Closed position @ 1280.21    = profit 178.78%

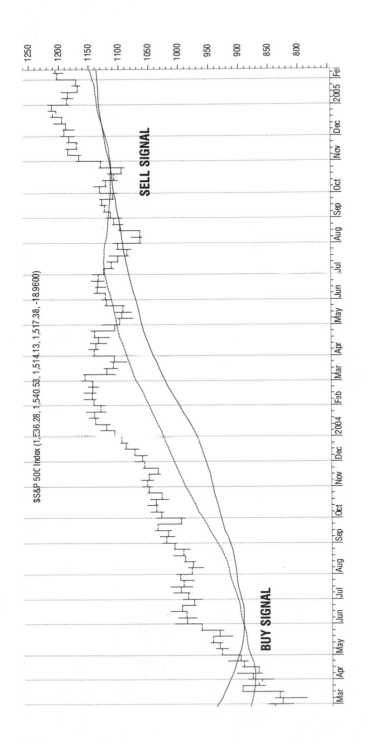

$S&P 50C Index (1,536.28, 1,540.53, 1,514.13, 1,517.38, -18.9600)

**SELL SIGNAL**

**BUY SIGNAL**

13 June 2003     Opened position @ 987.76

5 November 2004     Closed position @ 130.20     = profit 14.42%

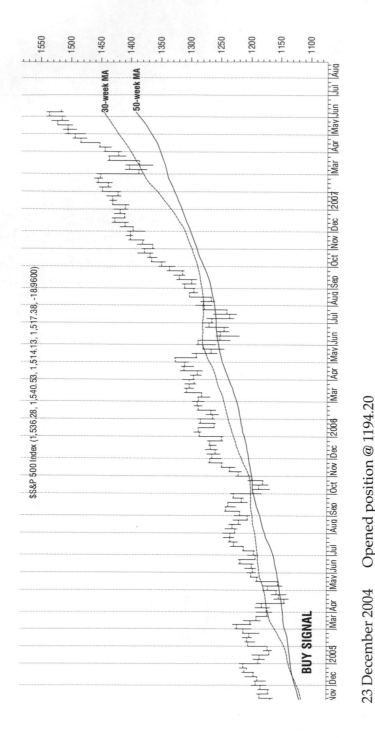

$S&P 500 Index (1,536.28, 1,540.53, 1,514.13, 1,514.13, 1,517.38, -18.9600)

30-week MA

50-week MA

BUY SIGNAL

23 December 2004    Opened position @ 1194.20
6 June 2007*        Market level @ 1517.38*        = profit 27.06%*

* This market position remained open as at the time the book went to print.

# S&P 500 Composite Index historical performance summary

The following summary includes the performance of the final market position, which remained open at the time the book went to print on 6 June 2007.

## *Summary of position*

| | | |
|---|---|---|
| 6 January 1951 | Opened position @ 20.77 | |
| 14 August 1953 | Closed position @ 24.75 | = profit 19.16% |
| | | |
| 5 March 1954 | Opened position @ 26.25 | |
| 8 February 1957 | Closed position @ 44.53 | = profit 69.64% |
| | | |
| 6 September 1957 | Opened position @ 45.44 | |
| 13 December 1957 | Closed position @ 40.92 | = (loss 9.95%) |
| | | |
| 25 July 1958 | Opened position @ 46.33 | |
| 4 March 1960 | Closed position @ 56.12 | = profit 21.13% |
| | | |
| 30 December 1960 | Opened position @ 57.52 | |
| 29 June 1962 | Closed position @ 52.45 | = (loss 8.81%) |
| | | |
| 15 March 1963 | Opened position @ 65.51 | |
| 22 July 1966 | Closed position @ 86.99 | = profit 32.79% |
| | | |
| 28 April 1967 | Opened position @ 92.62 | |
| 10 May 1968 | Closed position @ 98.35 | = profit 6.19% |
| | | |
| 21 June 1968 | Opened position @ 100.13 | |
| 11 July 1969 | Closed position @ 99.03 | = (loss 1.10%) |
| | | |
| 29 January 1971 | Opened position @ 95.28 | |
| 10 December 1971 | Closed position @ 96.51 | = profit 1.29% |
| | | |
| 24 March 1972 | Opened position @ 107.59 | |
| 13 July 1973 | Closed position @ 102.14 | = (loss 5.07%) |

| | | |
|---|---|---|
| 23 May 1975 | Opened position @ 90.53 | |
| 7 April 1977 | Closed position @ 98.23 | = profit 8.51% |
| | | |
| 25 August 1978 | Opened position @ 103.89 | |
| 12 April 1979 | Closed position @ 102.87 | = (loss 0.98%) |
| | | |
| 27 July 1979 | Opened position @ 101.59 | |
| 21 August 1981 | Closed position @ 131.66 | = profit 29.60% |
| | | |
| 12 November 1982 | Opened position @ 142.12 | |
| 23 March 1984 | Closed position @ 159.18 | = profit 12.00% |
| | | |
| 30 November 1984 | Opened position @ 166.90 | |
| 15 January 1988 | Closed position @ 243.46 | = profit 45.87% |
| | | |
| 2 September 1988 | Opened position @ 259.69 | |
| 29 June 1990 | Closed position @ 355.43 | = profit 36.87% |
| | | |
| 7 September 1990 | Opened position @ 322.56 | |
| 19 October 1990 | Closed position @ 300.03 | = (loss 6.98%) |
| | | |
| 10 May 1991 | Opened position @ 380.78 | |
| 15 July 1994 | Closed position @ 449.56 | = profit 18.06% |
| | | |
| 6 January 1995 | Opened position @ 459.21 | |
| 5 January 2001 | Closed position @ 1280.21 | = profit 178.78% |
| | | |
| 13 June 2003 | Opened position @ 987.76 | |
| 5 November 2004 | Closed position @ 1130.20 | = profit 14.42% |
| | | |
| 23 December 2004 | Opened position @ 1194.20 | |
| 6 June 2007* | Market level @ 1517.38* | = profit 27.06%* |

* This market position remained open as at the time the book went to print.

## *Summary of performance*

| | |
|---|---|
| Total number of positions held | 21 |
| Number of profitable positions | 15 |
| Percentage of profitable positions | 71.43% |
| Largest gain from a profitable position | 178.78% (1995 to 2001) |
| Average profit | 34.76% |
| Largest loss from a losing position | –9.95% (1957) |
| Average loss | –5.48% |
| Ratio of average profit/average loss | 6.3/1 |

As you can see from this historical record, with a total of just 41 signals (21 'buy' and 20 'sell') over the last 56 years, this is a very long-term approach to investing. Its strength is the ability to identify and participate in long-term bull market trends while also offering some protection against those vicious bear markets. As with any approach based on trend following, its weakness is that it requires these long-term trends to be profitable.

# 19

# The 1987 Crash

It would be remiss of me not to review one of the biggest sudden collapses of share values in modern history, namely the 1987 Crash, and how the System performed during the sell-off.

From the 1987 high of the S&P 500 Index to its lowest point, the index fell nearly 36 per cent, with most of those losses (around 28 per cent) occurring over just four days between 13 and 19 October, as shown in Figure 19.1.

As you should now be aware, the System is designed to participate in long-term bull trends and stay on the sidelines during long-term bear markets. Therefore, owing to its design, it tends to delay its reaction to shorter-term volatility. Generally, this is a positive attribute, as most of these price movements are pretty random in nature and are known in market terminology as 'noise'. Such price action typically has no effect on long-term trends, which is why the System contains no rules to react to it. However, there are always exceptions to the rule and the Crash was one of them.

On a positive note, prior to this big sell-off the stock market had been performing very strongly and was up approximately 39 per cent in the year to date. In fact, including the October Crash it may surprise you to learn that the S&P 500 still finished up on the year, as you can see in Figure 19.2.

The System entered 1987 in a buy mode and, despite the massive sell-off in October, maintained that buy mode throughout, ultimately posting a small profit on the year. To survive a 30 per cent drop in values and still end the year with a positive return is good, but it

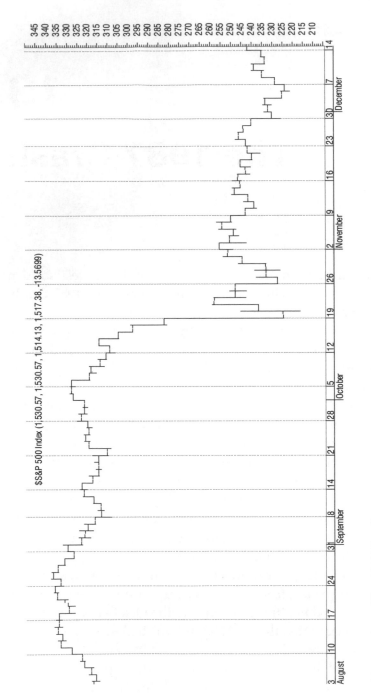

**Figure 19.1** The 1987 Crash

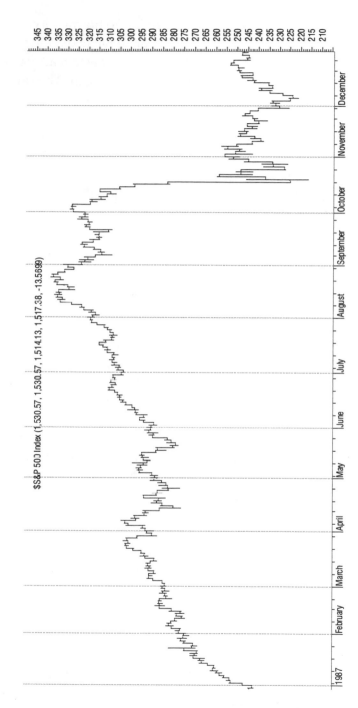

**Figure 19.2** Performance of the S&P 500 Index from 1 January to 31 December 1987

would have been a tough experience not dissimilar to the misfortune suffered by most investors that year. Had this price fall taken longer to unfold, the System would have undoubtedly had time to react, but the move was so quick it was almost over before it began. The fact that such a price movement is rare would have been no consolation at the time, but to put the move and the System's performance into perspective, it represented the loss of just that single year's unrealized profits (see Figure 19.2), and if you had been using the Long-Term Investment System at the time you would still have been sitting on unrealized profits of over 30 per cent since it originally went into buy mode.

# 20

# Conclusion

If you want to build a big pot of money to fund your retirement or children's education you are unlikely to achieve this by leaving your cash sitting in a savings account. To generate serious capital growth, you have to invest in stocks and shares.

(Harvey Jones, *Sunday Express*, 12 August 2007)

The profits generated by the Long-Term Investment System are the result of the unrelenting upward march of the stock market, a movement driven by large and diverse companies that are continually pushing the boundaries of technology, manufacturing, sales and productivity. It is a movement also driven by the billions of dollars, pounds and euros that pour into our pension funds month after month, which in turn are invested into the market. Any long-term chart of the stock market illustrates this upward momentum.

The System provides a disciplined way of participating in these profitable moves and contains rules that force you to adhere to the time-honoured investing maxim of 'running your profits and cutting your losses'. It certainly doesn't always work perfectly, but it works well enough for me to count on it. For many years, I have used the System to invest some of my own cash, and it has provided me with a steady string of profitable investments. In addition, I can continue with my life safe in the knowledge that, whenever a strong bull market trend occurs in stocks and shares, I will be participating and profiting from the move.

If you decide to follow the System and invest some of your own money into a stock market index, you are immediately diversifying your investment across the broad spectrum of stocks that make up that index. Additionally, you do not need to concern yourself with constantly monitoring the performance of individual stocks, because if one or two businesses begin to perform very badly they will be 'relegated' from the index at a periodical review and replaced by more strongly performing companies. For example, if we review how the component members of the FTSE 100 Index have changed since its inception in 1984, we can see how effective this portfolio management process is. Of the original 100 companies that made up the index, less than half are still in there. The remainder have merged, closed down or seen their performance superseded by that of some 'new', more strongly performing business. In fact, as I write this book, the FTSE Group, which is responsible for the construction of the index, has announced that, in its latest quarterly reshuffle, Daily Mail & General Trust PLC has been promoted back into the FTSE 100 at the expense of Cairn Energy, which has now been relegated. That's the beauty of operating with a stock market index: its focus is constantly changing and evolving as the world, business and technology change and evolve. By concentrating your stock market investment in an index, you are ensuring that your money is constantly invested in successful businesses, while old-fashioned and poorly performing companies can be dismissed. This regular 'promotion/relegation' review acts like a portfolio manager for you. Therefore, you only need to concern yourself with whether the long-term trend of the index is bullish or bearish and let the respective performance of the companies that make up the index decide whether or not they continue to remain in it.

As a stock market investor, you are faced with a multitude of investment options, including discretionary advice, investment newsletters, books, systems, actively managed funds, passive tracker funds, stock market indices, sectors or the individual stocks and shares themselves. Your choice of both strategy and investment vehicle will be dependent upon a number of factors, not least of which is your own personal level of expertise. You can apply the System in this book if you wish, you can develop one of your own or you can dismiss the whole argument of market timing. Whatever you decide to do, take your time to research how, when, where and with whom you are going to invest your money. And if you spend at least as much effort deliberating on your financial future as you would spend on the purchase of a new car, then you'll already be ahead of many private investors. A little effort is all you need to make *big money*, but you must do your homework first.

Market timing or systematic trend following, call it what you will, provides an investor with the opportunity to participate in the strongest bull market trends, but, more importantly, offers protection from the most severe long-term bear markets. It is a risk management strategy. You wouldn't or shouldn't drive a car without a seat belt, just in case something goes wrong, and likewise you shouldn't place your cash at risk in the stock market without at least having some form of protection in case the market enters a long period of poor performance. Nothing in life is perfect, and a timing approach cannot completely eliminate risk, nor does it guarantee to provide immunity from losses, but it does seek to protect you from the worst effects of a sustained rundown in values and in doing so allows you to live to fight another day. Recessions, depressions and bear markets are a fact of life, and your goal as an investor is to ride such storms. Not only will this mean that, when a new bull market develops, you will have a great deal more of your capital available to invest compared to an investor who would have remained invested throughout a decline in prices, but you will also be more likely to participate in the new trend because psychologically your recent experience of the stock market will bear no resemblance to the stress experienced by investors who, as many do, stay invested all the way down.

In summary, the Long-Term Investment System performs particularly well when applied to the stock market via the use of stock market indices. It's where I put some of my money, and it's where I recommend you should consider placing some of yours.

Thank you for your time, and I wish you every success.

# Appendix A
## Useful contacts

## United Kingdom

**Financial Ombudsman Service**
South Quay Plaza
183 Marsh Wall
London E14 9SR
Consumer helpline: 0845 080 1800
www.financial-ombudsman.org.uk

**Financial Services Authority (FSA)**
25 The Colonnade
Canary Wharf
London E14 5HS
Consumer helpline (from United Kingdom): 0845 606 1234
Consumer helpline (from overseas): +44 20 7066 1000
www.fsa.gov.uk

**Independent Financial Advice Guide**
Manor Coach House
Church Hill
Aldershot
Hampshire GU12 4RQ
www.ifa-guide.co.uk

# United States

**Securities and Exchange Commission (SEC)**
100 F Street, NE
Washington, DC 20549
Investor information: www.sec.gov / investor.shtml

# Appendix B

# Stock market index investment products

## Tracker funds

These unleveraged mutual funds and unit trusts are a relatively recent addition to the fund management world. Essentially they invest their portfolios with the objective of matching the performance of the underlying index they track. The fund management companies that operate such funds do this by using a variety of methods, such as buying the shares in all the companies that make up the underlying index, buying the shares of selected companies they feel best represent the index or, alternatively, using exotic financial instruments such as derivatives. Although the concept of tracking an index sounds straightforward, owing to the variety of investment options available to a fund management company each tracker fund will have a different performance record, and some of the less well-managed trackers have been known to underperform their respective index by as much as 15 per cent, which rather defeats the objective of using one! As with all products offered by the fund management community, these funds are subject to fees, but they are typically not that high, as the time spent on management is minimal, with the only adjustments needed to a funds portfolio governed by the monthly inflows and outflows of investors' money or a change to the composition of the index the funds are attempting to track. On an annual basis, the performance of a good tracker fund should not be far away from the performance of its underlying index.

As I've mentioned before, if you're still unsure which fund suits your needs best, a competent recommended independent financial adviser (IFA) should be able to provide you with a list of all the tracker funds that cover the index you want to invest in. When reviewing this list, pay particular attention to those funds that appear the most accurate at replicating the performance of their underlying index over the long term. Your financial adviser should also be able to provide you with additional information such as the management fees charged and the minimum investment required.

## Exchange traded funds (ETFs)

The first exchange traded fund was launched in Canada in 1990 and three years later in the United States. Eventually exchange traded funds arrived in the United Kingdom in 2000 and now ETFs, to give them their popular acronym, are an accepted part of the financial universe. Effectively an ETF is a financial product that tracks a specific index or basket of assets but is traded on an exchange like a single stock. Because ETFs are index-linked rather than actively managed and have a constantly changing intra-day value driven by the price changes of the underlying index or basket of assets they are tracking, they appeal to both professional and private investors. As ETFs trade on a stock exchange, each transaction is subject to a broker's commission, but on the positive side there are no financial adviser kickbacks on sales. Exchange traded funds offer investors a low-cost opportunity to participate in an index and are a viable investment option.

# Appendix C

## Top 20 largest stock exchanges

The largest stock exchanges as at May 2007 (by market capitalization, in trillions of US dollars) were:

1. NYSE Euronext – $20.69
2. Tokyo Stock Exchange – $4.68
3. NASDAQ – $4.16
4. London Stock Exchange – $4.02
5. Toronto Stock Exchange – $1.99
6. Frankfurt Stock Exchange (Deutsche Börse) – $1.97
7. Hong Kong Stock Exchange – $1.92
8. Shanghai Stock Exchange – $1.79
9. Madrid Stock Exchange (BME Spanish Exchanges) – $1.52
10. Australian Securities Exchange – $1.32
11. Swiss Exchange – $1.32
12. Nordic Stock Exchange Group OMX – $1.30
13. Milan Stock Exchange (Borsa Italiana) – $1.12
14. Bombay Stock Exchange – $1.01
15. Korea Exchange – $1.00
16. São Paulo Stock Exchange Bovespa – $0.98
17. National Stock Exchange of India – $0.96
18. Moscow Interbank Currency Exchange – $0.86 (January 2007)
19. Johannesburg Securities Exchange – $0.80
20. Taiwan Stock Exchange – $0.61

(*Source:* World Federation of Exchanges, June 2007)

# Glossary of financial terms

Here is a brief glossary of financial and market terminology:

**advisory broker**  A broker who imparts his or her wisdom to clients, who pay a higher brokerage commission rate for this knowledge and expertise.

**analysts**  Individuals who work for financial institutions such as banks and brokerage houses. Their job is to analyse and report upon various aspects of an investment and offer their opinion regarding its future profitability.

**annual charge (also management fee)**  A fee charged by a fund management company and usually levied as a fixed percentage of the amount of money the company manages for a client.

**ask price (also offer price)**  The price at which investors can buy.

**asset**  Anything that is of value to anyone, for example stocks and shares, property, bonds, vintage cars, antiques, etc.

**bar chart**  Technical analysis term for a chart that graphically represents as vertical bars the open, high, low and closing prices for a specified period.

**bear**  Someone who believes that market prices will fall.

**bear market**  A market where prices are falling.

**bid–ask spread (also bid–offer spread)**  The difference between the prices of an asset or market at which investors can buy or sell. The 'bid' is always the lower price and the 'ask' is always the higher price. The greater the difference between the bid and the ask prices, the more expensive it is for an investor to participate.

**bid–offer spread (also bid–ask spread)**   The difference between the prices of an asset or market at which investors can buy or sell. The 'bid' is always the lower price and the 'offer' is always the higher price. The greater the difference between the bid and the offer prices, the more expensive it is for an investor to participate.

**bid price**   The price at which investors can sell.

**blue chip**   Market terminology for a large, well-capitalized company.

**brokerage**   The commission charged by a broker to a client for executing a transaction.

**brokerage account**   A broker account that requires the client to 'deposit' cash with the company before any positions can be established.

**bull**   Someone who believes that market prices will rise.

**bull market**   A market where prices are rising.

**buy and hold**   A strategy that involves establishing and maintaining a stock market investment until a specified monetary target or time frame has been reached.

**capital gain**   The appreciation in the value of an investment.

**compounding**   The beneficial effect upon the appreciation of an investment as a direct result of the reinvestment of profits from that same investment.

**day trading**   The practice of short-term trading where speculators (day traders) attempt to profit from price movements occurring over minutes or hours. All positions are typically closed by the end of trading each day, with no position held overnight.

**dividend**   A payment made to shareholders, usually quarterly, out of a company's current or retained earnings. Dividends can be paid in either stock or cash.

**exchange traded fund (ETF)**   A financial product that tracks a specific index or basket of assets but is traded on an exchange like a single stock.

**execution-only broker**   A broker who simply executes the buy and sell instructions of clients without offering any opinions or advice. Typically the execution-only broker's commission will be lower than that of other types of broker.

**Financial Ombudsman** A body that acts as an arbitrator in complaints and disputes between financial companies and individuals.

**Financial Services Authority (FSA)** A UK government body empowered under the Financial Services Act to regulate the financial services industry.

**financial services provider** A regulated company whose business is to manage client monies invested in financial products sold either directly to the public or through a regulated financial adviser.

**front load (also initial charge)** A one-off fee charged to investors when they initially invest in certain financial products.

**fundamental analysis** A method of analysis that generally focuses upon data concerning supply and demand and economic statistics.

**independent financial adviser (IFA)** A regulated financial adviser who can sell the investment products of numerous financial service providers.

**initial charge (also front load)** A one-off fee charged to investors when they initially invest in certain financial products.

**internet broker (also online broker)** A broker who accepts buy and sell instructions from clients via the internet.

**investment capital** An amount of money that can be invested free from the demands of daily, weekly, monthly or annual living expenses.

**leverage** Terminology for the ability to control an amount of money greater than the amount of cash employed.

**liquidity** Terminology for any market where there are numerous buyers and sellers competing, thus making it easier to establish or close a position near the current market price.

**long** Terminology for a position that is established with a 'buy' order and benefits from an upward movement in prices.

**long term** My interpretation is any time period greater than a calendar week.

**management fee (also annual charge)** A fee charged by a fund management company and usually levied as a fixed percentage of the amount of money the company manages for a client.

**margin call**   A request made by a broker to a client to immediately deposit cash to cover some or all of the client's exposure to loss.

**market maker**   A financial institution that will 'make' a price in an investment by quoting a bid–offer spread, thereby accepting the other side of an investor's purchase or sale.

**market timing**   An investment strategy that generates buy and sell signals based upon the premise that an upward trend in stock market prices, once established, has a high probability of maintaining that momentum.

**mechanical system**   A system that provides buy and sell signals generated by predetermined rules.

**moving average (MA)**   Technical analysis term for a tool that averages market closing prices for a specific period.

**offer price (also ask price)**   The price at which investors can buy.

**online broker (also internet broker)**   A broker who accepts buy and sell instructions from clients via the internet.

**risk**   In the context of this book, the amount or the probability of an investment losing money.

**short**   Terminology for a position that is established with a 'sell' order and benefits from a downward movement in prices.

**short term**   My interpretation is any time period less than a calendar week.

**technical analysis**   The study of market price action through the use of charts.

**tied adviser**   A regulated financial adviser who is only permitted to sell the investment products of one financial services provider.

**tracker fund**   A fund that attempts to match the performance of a specified market index.

**trend**   The sustained movement of market prices in a given direction (up or down).

**trend-following system**   A system that generates buy and sell signals based upon the premise that a trend in prices, once established, has a high probability of maintaining that momentum.

**unrealized gain/profit**   The appreciation in value of an investment that has not, as yet, been sold (liquidated).

**unrealized loss**   The depreciation in value of an investment that has not, as yet, been sold (liquidated).

# References and further reading

Covel, Michael (2004) *Trend-Following*, Financial Times Prentice Hall, New York

Dent, Harry (1993) *The Great Boom Ahead*, Hyperion, New York

Dent, Harry (1998) *The Roaring 2000s*, Simon & Schuster, New York

Dent, Harry (1999) *The Roaring 2000s Investor*, Simon & Schuster, New York

Edwards, Robert and Magee, John (1992) *Technical Analysis of Stock Trends*, New York Institute of Finance, New York

Fisher, P A (1996) *Common Stocks and Uncommon Profits*, John Wiley & Sons, New York

Koch, Richard (1997) *The 80/20 Principle*, Nicholas Brealey Publishing, London

Lynch, P (2000) *One Up on Wall Street*, Fireside, New York

Murphy, John (1986) *Technical Analysis of the Futures Markets*, New York Institute of Finance, New York

O'Higgins, Michael (2000) *Beating the Dow*, HarperCollins, New York

Pilzer, Paul Zane (1995) *God Wants You to Be Rich*, Simon & Schuster, New York

Plummer, Tony (2006) *Forecasting Financial Markets*, Kogan Page, London

Schwager, Jack (1989) *Market Wizards*, New York Institute of Finance, New York

Schwager, Jack (1992) *The New Market Wizards*, New York Institute of Finance, New York

Taleb, Nassim Nicholas (2001) *Fooled by Randomness*, Texere, New York

Zweig, Marty (1997) *Winning on Wall Street*, Warner Books, New York

# Index

NB: page numbers in *italic* indicate figures

1987 crash   149–52

advisers, independent financial
     13, 97, 101
advisers, tied   12
'amateur' investors   23–24
analysts   11 12
asset allocation (and)   87–88,
     *89*, 90–101
  individual stocks and
       shares/sectors   97, *98*,
       *99, 100*
  level of investment   101
  market risk   87–88
  security risk   88
  stock market index timing
       91–92, *93, 94*, 95, *96*, 97

banks   13–14
  and commissioned selling
       13
bar charts *see* charts: operating
     the System

bear market   48, *49*, 51, 54,
     56–57, 87, 92, *94*
*Beating the Dow*   38
beating the professionals
     21–24 *see also* 'amateur'
     investors
Bolton, A   90
brokers   11–12
Buffet, W   10
bull and bear trends   51–52
bull market   35, 42, 57, 65, 75,
     87, 92, *93*
buy-and-hold *see* market timing
buying low, selling high   33–34

CAC 40 Index (France)   116–17
charts: operating the System
     77, *78*, 78, *79*, 79, *80, 81,*, 82,
     *83, 84*, 85, *86*
Cheval, L   69
cold calls   16
commission-based income   17
company collapses   48

computers, advantages of
42–43
Covel, M   46
creation of traders / investors:
Turtles experiment   67–69

Dax 30 Index (Germany)   90,
91, 115–16
Dennis, R   67–69
disciplined market timing *see*
market timing
Donchian, R   71–73
dotcom.boom   49
Dow, C H   91–92
Dow Jones Industrial Average
(USA)   38, 88, 90, 91–92,
111–12
due diligence questions   16–18

Eckhardt, B   67–68
Edwards, R   77
emotional intelligence (EQ)
34–35
Enron   11
evaluating systems, benefits of
41–44

failure, reasons for   25–35
assumptions   30–31
buying low, selling high
33–34
fear and greed   34–35
goal-setting   26–27
lack of planning   28–30
need for perfection   32–33
procrastination   31–32
Faith, C   69
figures
bar chart 78

bar chart with moving
averages   79
bear market (1973–74)   49
bear market trend   94
BHP Billiton (June 2003–
December 2006)   100
British Airways (July
1991–August 1994)   98
bull market trend   93
comparative performance of
buy and hold vs market
timing (1995–2007)   55
futuresource.com charge
page: stock index
information   83
futuresource.com chart page:
moving average study
84
futuresource.com charts page
81
futuresource.com final weekly
chart   86
futuresource.com home page
80
market-timing equity profile
96
NASDAQ Index (October 1998
to September 2001)   50
performance of Microsoft vs
Dow Jones Industrial
Average   89
S&P 500 Index 1995–2007)
53
Sear Roebuck (March 1995–
December 1996)   99
financial planning   28–30
following a system *see* signals
*and* system, psychology of
following a

*Fooled by Randomness* 42
*Forecasting Financial Markets*
26
*Fortune* 20
friends and foes 15–19
FTSE 100 Index (UK) 88, 90, 91,
114–15
Fuller, D 57
fund managers 10–11
country-/continent-specific
22
and specialization 21–22
successful *see* Turtles, the

goals, setting 26–27

Hang Seng Index (Hong Kong)
90, 121–22
hedge fund management 1, 4,
22, 24, 32, 37, 64
historical performance of system
123–47
Hite, L 32
humility 31

independent financial advisers
(IFAs) 13, 97, 101
index tracking products 97
investment management and
the amateur 23–24

KISS strategies 63–65

Long-Term Investment System
2–4, 5–6, 39, 44, 51–52, 54,
61, 64, 65, 69, 71–73, 95–96,
153–55
and 1987 crash 149, *150, 151,*
152

charts for operating 77, *78,*
*78, 79, 79, 80, 81,* 82, *83,*
*84,* 85, *86*
and company shares 97
rules for 75–76
'low-risk' investments
18–19
Lynch, P 23

Magee, J 77
*Mail on Sunday* 39
'Dogs of the Footsie' 39
market risk 87–88
market timing
disciplined 45–46
vs buy and hold 47–49, *49,*
*50,* 51–52, *53,* 54, *55,*
56–57
market falls in value 56
Metastock software 43–44, 85
*see also* websites
Microsoft (MSFT) 88
mis-selling 12, 13
Motley Fool website 38, 47
and 'Foolish Four' method
38–39
moving averages (MA)
72–73
Murphy, J 77

NASDAQ-100 Composite Index
(USA) 49, 56, 91, 112–13
*Next Big Investment Boom, The*
2, 3
Nikkei 225 Index (Japan) 88,
91, 117–21

O'Higgins, M 38, 39
*One Up on Wall Street* 23

operational guide *see* charts:
Long-Term Investment
System *and* operating the
System

Parker, J   69
perfection, searching for
32–33
planning and focusing   28–30
Plummer, T   26, 27
price level prediction   33–34

questions to ask   16–18

Rabar, P   69
reasons for saving and
investment   7–8
research on managed funds
90
retirement, saving for   7
risk *see* market risk *and* security
risk
rules for investment   75–76

S&P Composite Index *see*
Standard & Poor's 500
Composite Index (USA)
salespeople and investment
16–17
security risk   88
signals   60–61, 65, 75–76
anticipating   60
buy   75, 76, 95
and listening to 'armchair
investors'   61
sell   60, 75, 76, 95
system   60
simplicity   63–65
stage analysis   3

Standard & Poor's 500
Composite Index (USA)
51–52, *53*, 54, 56, 88, 91,
103–10
historical performance
summary   145–47
historical record   123, *124–44*
statistical and system analysis
64 *see also* charts: operating
the System
stock exchanges, top 20 largest
161
stock market index investment
products   159–60
stock market indices   91–92,
103–22
CAC 40 Index (France)
116–17
Dax 30 Index (Germany)   90,
91, 115–16
Dow Jones Industrial Average
(USA)   38, 88, 90, 91–92,
111–12
FTSE 100 Index (UK)   88, 90,
91, 114–15
Hang Seng Index (Hong
Kong)   90, 121–22
NASDAQ-100 Composite
Index (USA)   49, 56, 91,
112–13
Nikkei   225 Index (Japan) 88,
91, 117–21
Standard & Poor's 500
Composite Index (USA)
88, 91, 103–10
stock markets   75–76 *see also*
signals
Asian   22
Japanese   22, 48

system, psychology of following 59–61 *see also* signals
and falling into traps 60–61
systematic investing 37–39

Taleb, N N 42
*Technical Analysis of Stock Trends* 77
*Technical Analysis of the Futures Markets* 77
telephone calls, unsolicited 16
tied advisers 12
Tilley, D 65
Trelford, D 16
*Trend-Following* 46
trend-following strategies 46, 51
trust (and) 9–14
brokers/analysts 11–12

fund managers 10–11
independent financial advisers 13
other professionals 13–14
tied advisers 12
Turtles, the 67–69

useful contacts 157–58

*Wall Street Journal / Customer's Afternoon Letter* 92
websites
Equis International: www.equis.com 43
Paritech: www.paritech.co.uk 44
*Winning on Wall Street* 38

Zweig, M 38